S0-ABB-610

David Graham with Danny Acret

David Graham's Guide to Golf Equipment

Charles E. Tuttle Company, Inc.
Boston • Rutland, Vermont • Tokyo

First published in the United States in 1993 by
Charles E. Tuttle Company, Inc. of Rutland,
Vermont & Tokyo, Japan, with editorial offices
at 77 Central Street, Boston, Massachusetts 02109.

Drawings by Joyce Tulkens

*Cover Illustration: David Graham on his new golf
course at Laguna Quays, Whitsundays, Australia
(Photograph by Peter Beattie)*

Library of Congress Catalog Card Number 92-62858

ISBN 0-8048-1848-7

Typeset by Superskill Graphics Pte. Ltd.
PRINTED IN SINGAPORE

To all people who love the game of golf and want to understand it

ACKNOWLEDGEMENTS

The publisher wishes to thank adidas AG and TI Apollo Ltd. for kindly supplying information and Palmer Golf (Singapore) Pte. Ltd. for lending equipment for the art work.

CONTENTS

FOREWORD

There is one special club in every golfer's bag which over time has become a favourite. After years of wear it often looks like an heirloom from grandfather, decrepit and weather-beaten, with rust spots and in need of repair, but rarely will a player part with it.

My long-time favourite is my putter. I bought it some thirty years ago in Japan. It was a no-name brand and very cheap. Yet I have used this putter throughout my career and it has brought me countless victories in major tournaments around the world, to become the single most significant club in my collection.

Arriving at Augusta National or the site of another championship to find either my putter broken or lost was my worst nightmare. I can't remember when I told David Graham about it. Our friendship goes back a long way, practising and playing together on the tour. David immediately offered to make a working replica of my putter, and I was stunned by the result. It was simply outstanding, and I still use the putter today.

David was always like that. He would go out of his way to help fellow golfers, even his competitors. And he is a real expert. Shortly after starting his golfing career at the age of fourteen, David began tinkering with clubs. He developed his skills working with some of the best known golf manufacturers in the world, and today he is an eminent club designer.

Of course, David is also an illustrious golfer. From humble beginnings as a caddie he became the only Australian to win both the U.S. Open and the U.S. PGA. Through his dedication and determination, he learned to understand golf inside and out. As far as I am concerned David is the best possible author for this book.

I don't know if you have a favourite putter as I do or if you cherish another club in your bag. But chances are you will learn a thing or two about it from David. Whether choosing a new set of clubs, upgrading your old set, or simply selecting a new brand of golf balls, this book will prove invaluable. It is an accessible, easy to understand guide for the golfing public on just about everything you always wanted to know about golf equipment, but didn't know who to ask.

This book will be a great help to golfers of all ages and levels of achievement, who love the game as I do, and strive continuously to master it.

Gary Player

DANNY ACRET ABOUT DAVID GRAHAM

The first time I saw David Graham he was an unheralded 22-year-old professional. It was Easter 1968, in my home town of Forbes in the central west of New South Wales. Our club was hosting the Australian Junior Interstate Teams' Series. Graham had accompanied a friend, and used the opportunity to practise during the four days of the tournament.

I was eleven years old and one of the caddies for the NSW team, busy with my player but every time I was around the practice fairway, Graham was there hitting wedge shots . . . . just wedge shots, nothing else . . . . all day, every day. I remember watching Graham, absorbed in the skill of his shotmaking. What I should have been studying was his work ethic. I now know that was the key to his many achievements in golf.

At the time, Graham was an emerging talent, who two years later was catapulted to stardom when he teamed with Bruce Devlin to win the World Cup in Buenos Aires, Graham finishing second to Roberto de Vicenzo in the individual championship.

Through the next dozen years, Graham established himself as one of Australia's greatest golfers and certainly the most successful to compete in the United States. He defeated Ben Crenshaw for the 1979 U.S. PGA, and took out the 1981 U.S. Open. His closing 67, in which he missed only one fairway and hit every green in regulation at Merion to win the Open was described by Ben Hogan as the greatest final round by the winner of a major championship, and *U.S. Golf Digest* voted it the Round of the Decade.

In 1977 our paths crossed for a second time when I competed in the Australian Open at The Australian Golf Club. Graham was an exempt player while I gained a start through the qualifying events, and our pre-tournament status was reflected in the scoring. Graham won his national championship for the only time while I missed the cut.

I suppose it's under those circumstances that you realize how much hard work can do for your game. In my case, as an amateur golfer with no great ambitions, I realized how much work I had not done on my game.

Graham, the winner, however, had worked harder than anyone to succeed. The story of David Graham is an extraordinary one, that of an iron-willed boy who set his sights on reaching the pinnacle of his sport and overcoming one obstacle after another.

Nothing came easy. Aged twelve, Graham had started to play golf with old clubs he had found at home. Never mind that they were left hander's clubs, and he was a right hander. Soon, he was playing to a 1-handicap.

After he came home from school, he worked at the local pro shop, sweeping the floors, and putting in long hours over the weekends. It was there that he gained his first knowledge of golf equipment. He reshafted clubs, changed the plates on the club soles, fitted new grips, and laid the foundation for his future in club design.

Against his father's wishes, he became an apprentice professional at the age of 14, and has hardly seen his father since, or his sister. He did the dirty work in the pro shop for 15 or 16 hours a day, and started assembling the clubs from bins full of clubheads, shafts and grips, trying them out, and pulling them apart again, until they felt right for the customers.

At that stage, he also manufactured there his own first right-handed set. It took Graham two years of hitting balls at odd hours of the day before and after work to complete the change from the left to the right hand. But today he is convinced that his great success as a player would not have been possible any other way.

As a young professional, Graham took a job in Tasmania, but he was still an inexperienced teenager, and wound up broke and in debt before his 20th birthday. Although his iron work discipline and his meticulous techniques as a tournament player quickly set him back on his feet, an unfortunate association with an American manager left him almost penniless again in the mid 1970s.

In 1965, Graham joined Precision Golf Forgings, fitting custom clubs, working with loft-and-lie machines, of

The Victories

1967 Queensland PGA
1970 Tasmanian Open
Victorian Open
Thailand Open
French Open
Yomiori Open
World Cup (with Bruce Devlin)
1971 Caracas Open
Japanese Airlines Open
1972 Cleveland Open
1975 Wills Masters
1976 Chunichi Crown
Westchester Classic
American Golf Classic
Piccadilly World Match Play
1977 Australian Open
1978 Mexico Cup
1979 US PGA Championship
West Lakes Classic
Air New Zealand Open
1980 Memorial Tournament
Heublin Classic
Rolex World Mixed Teams' Championship (with Jan Stephenson)
Mexican Open
1981 Phoenix Open
US Open
Lancome Trophy
1982 Lancome Trophy
1983 Houston Open
1985 Queensland Open
1987 Queensland Open

which he later would design his own model, and learning more about the research and development of golf clubs. Before and after work, rain or shine he would hit golf balls, hundreds or a thousand a day. It wasn't until 1971 that he became friends with Jack Nicklaus, and started to design clubs for MacGregor. By then, he was also well on his way to success as a player.

Even on the tour, Graham carried his little tool bag around, filled with bits and pieces to tinker with equipment and repair clubs when they were needed most. Tournament professionals like Greg Norman, came to appreciate his expertise and hands-on approach. More recently he designed the Daiwa Advisor 273 irons used by Ian Baker-Finch to win the 1991 British Open at Royal Birkdale. Incidentally, the 273 stands for Graham's winning score in the 1981 U.S. Open.

I, like many young golf fans, followed David Graham's career from afar. To us he appeared to be a highly successful player enjoying a glamorous life style. It was not until much later that I learned the truth, and began to wonder how he ever managed to keep going, and how many people in those same circumstances would have given up.

Co-authoring this book proved quite an intimidating experience at times, because of the sheer amount of knowledge David Graham has gathered throughout a lifetime, although I spent the past five years putting together the Australian Golf Digest and reviewing new equipment for the magazine.

I had become wildly interested in everything related to golf right after I first picked up a golf club aged four. While my classmates dreamed about a new bike or a cricket bat, I dreamed about a full matched set of clubs and would discuss at length club specifications, shafts, persimmon heads, balata and surlyn balls.

I never became the professional golfer I hoped to be, but still play to a two handicap. As editor of Golf Digest I enjoy discussing the finer points of equipment with tournament players and club professionals, although the work leaves me little time to fiddle with clubs as much as I used to do.

Researching this book gave me ample opportunity to expand my knowledge about equipment and gain more insight into the life of David Graham. In clubhouses, pro shops and on the tournament circuit I found him held in great esteem and respected much beyond my expectations, as a player, a coach and an expert on equipment.

SHOPPING FOR EQUIPMENT

For most golfers, the pro shop is the adult equivalent of a candy store. Like you and me, they love to look and tinker with new equipment, and often end up buying whether they actually planned to purchase or not. Golfers are genuinely fascinated by their sport, and it shows.

Part of the attraction is the ever-growing range of equipment on the market. I can't think of any other sport that requires as many tools as ours. There are different clubs for all the shots on the course and for all players, from the novice to the professional. Golfing tools and toys account for a multi-billion-dollar business every year, and it continues to grow in volume and in variety.

Playing equipment has become so specialized that most golfers have only a superficial knowledge of club designs. Even the advertisement of club manufacturers today is far too technical to be understood by the majority of players. They buy a particular club because Nick Faldo or another superstar plays it, or because their foursome-partner outdrives them with his new wood, but they don't consider that Faldo is in a different league altogether and that their playing partner is separated from them by handicap, build and golf swing. Very few people know what works best for them.

Golfers are as diverse as the equipment designed for them, and that is why there is no such thing as the best set of clubs in the world. There are plenty of good clubs around, and quite a few not so good ones as well, but they are all designed for specific tasks and specific players, and they are good or bad only in relation to this task. A club that is good for me is not necessarily good for you.

Before a club is created on the drawing board, the clubmaker is given the requirements and specifications for a particular piece of equipment. A club is always designed for somebody, never anybody. In practice, this means that a particular set of clubs is tailored for very low handicappers for instance, or for high handicappers for that matter. You need to find the one that is made for you.

Had you and I met in person, we would have taken a stroll to the driving range, you would have shown me your swing, and I would have told you what equipment you need. Reading this book is your second best bet.

I will analyse one by one the different components of the club much as I did when I used to design them. You will find yourself in one or several of the different groups of golfers that I recommend equipment for, whether you are an average handicapper without a lot of power or a low handicap player with a strong swing.

Distance For An Average Golfer

CLUBS	YARDS
1-Wood	205
2-Wood	195
3-Wood	185
4-Wood	175
5-Wood	165
1-Iron	185
2-Iron	175
3-Iron	165
4-Iron	155
5-Iron	145
6-Iron	135
7-Iron	125
8-Iron	115
9-Iron	105
Pitching Wedge	95
Sand Wedge	85

You will find out if your current clubs are made for you or if you would be well advised to go and visit the pro shop. What you and I don't know is if your new clubs will help you play better golf. If you don't take them to the practice range or if your swing is faulty, you can't expect them to bail you out.

Amateurs try very hard to find the one club and the one ball that allows them to gain more distance. Now, golf is already the one sport in which the ball is propelled farther than in any other. And the Rules of Golf wisely limit the flight of golf balls so that our courses are not becoming obsolete. Before we delve into the details of clubfitting, look at the table on page 21 to see what distances an average male golfer can reasonably expect from each club.

Mind you, these distances are just broad guidelines. You will have to consider the conditions you are playing in. You can easily subtract ten yards each for wind, fog, cold weather and an elevated green. You will easily gain, with or without new clubs, about ten yards each in dry climates, high altitudes and warm weather.

If you want to go one step further, many pro shops now offer facilities to measure your clubhead speed, ball speed, the trajectory of your ball and the backspin you generate. This may be a sobering experience, but I think getting to know one's golfing self is a good start towards a better game.

Clubhead speeds range from 70 mph for ladies to 90 mph for an average male golfer and 110 mph for a professional. Considering that a swing arc is roughly thirty feet long, it is not surprising that most players don't find the sweet spot at impact as often as they wish. But it is the combination of both the clubhead speed and the angle at which the clubface meets the ball that decides how fast and how far the ball travels. The initial velocity of the ball generated with a driver can vary between 90 mph and 150 mph.

These numbers may help you to put your swing style into perspective, if you are not very sure about your abilities. The person who should be able to answer your questions is the professional. He or she should also be your first consultant when shopping for equipment. Your coach will be in the best position to give you a second opinion on your swing, and he has all the gadgets to fiddle with your clubs and to test new equipment.

This book is only the start. The advice you will find in the following pages is meant to give you a basic knowledge of how equipment works together and how it reacts to your swing. The rest is up to you. I would like to see you play to the best of your abilities. And while new equipment may not cure your slice if your swing is at fault, it just may if your clubs did not fit your swing. Whatever your handicap, you need equipment that suits your skills to work towards a better game.

CLUBHEAD SHAPES

Choosing the right clubheads is becoming increasingly difficult because of the vast range of models available. Classic shapes slowly disappear and make room for carefully engineered forms with specific functions. A couple of years ago, it appeared that clubhead materials dictated the shape they were to take, as not all functions could be incorporated into all materials. But today technology has advanced to a stage where you can choose your favourite clubhead shape and buy it in almost any material you fancy.

There are basically two things you want to be mindful of in choosing your clubhead shape. The first and foremost is aesthetics. In other words, you must like what you see. You can purchase the most expensive, game-improvement club you can find, but unless you like the looks of it, it won't do your game any good. Golf is as much a game of the mind as it is of the body, if not more so, that is why your clubs must make you feel comfortable and give you confidence.

The other consideration is, of course, compatibility. Golf clubs today are precision tools, designed with special groups of handicappers in mind. And like good tools, good golf clubs are quite useless unless you can handle them. As a rule of thumb, the lower your handicap, the bigger your choice in the pro shop, and vice versa. I will try to help you eliminate all those clubs that are not right for you. Let's look at the shape of woods first.

Classic Drivers and Fairway Woods

You know, of course, that the shafts of your driver and fairway woods are longer than those of your irons, providing you with a wider swing arc, and more clubhead speed. But the wider arc also means that your clubhead has to travel farther to reach the ball at impact, which in turn makes it less likely that you hit the ball precisely every time. To compensate for this inaccuracy, club manufacturers started years ago to produce drivers and woods with an expanded sweet spot.

The sweet spot is actually the area of the clubface with which the ball should ideally be struck at impact for a straight and high trajectory. In the traditional wooden clubs the mass of the material, and thus the weight, is concentrated behind the sweet spot. This allows good golfers to play very efficiently with the classic clubs.

Perimeter-Weighted Woods

To increase the sweet spot for golfers of lesser ability, club manufacturers manipulated the weight of the clubs. Metal soles and inserts were used in traditional

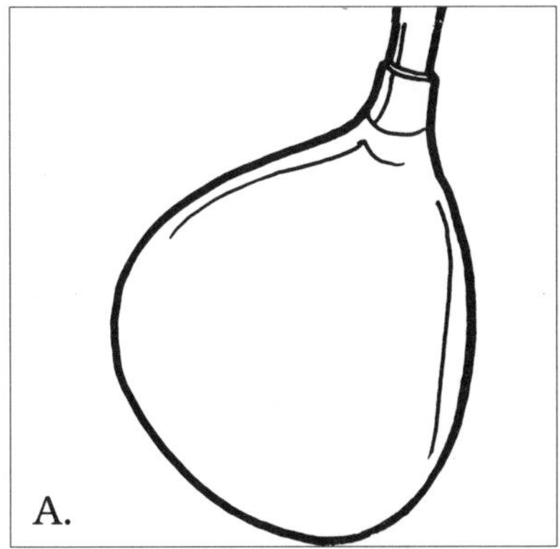

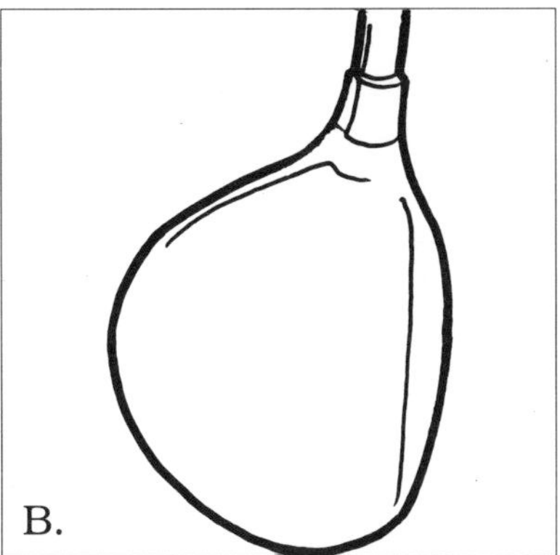

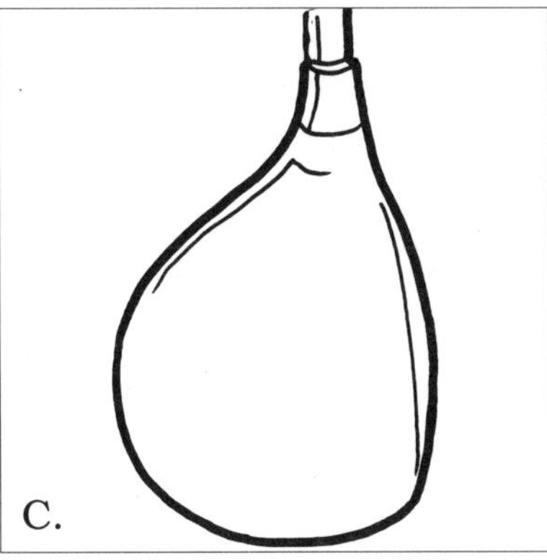

A. This is the new oversized variety with a bigger hitting area than any other club. B. Most new clubs on the market are midsized, although the sweet spot is still large. C. Classic clubs look slim and slender in comparison.

woods to lower the centre of gravity, which in turn helps to improve the clubhead speed and to get the ball airborne.

Clubmakers experimented first with heel-to-toe weighing in the 1960s. As it turned out, this feature actually helped to correct the flight of mis-hit balls, but it proved not good enough, and the perimeter-weighted club was invented.

In the perimeter-weighted clubhead, the weight is distributed around the edges of the club, providing golfers with a larger sweet spot and a more forgiving club. Although the first of these clubs were metal-headed woods, today there are even perimeter-weighted persimmon woods on the market, in which the clubhead is filled with a lighter material.

Oversized Perimeter-Weighted Woods

To extend the hitting area, the clubface became longer, and the head more prominent and bigger. Modern clubheads are up to twice the size of conventional models. The first oversized club that captured the public's imagination was Callaway's stainless steel-headed Big Bertha. Ever since clubmakers have struggled to keep up with demand.

Although I don't believe that the oversized perimeter-weighted wood allows you to hit the ball farther, it certainly lets your mis-hit ball travel in a straighter line. However, if the clubhead is very large, the aerodynamics may work against you, and lower your clubhead speed, thereby undoing at least some of the advantages you tried to gain with this sort of club in the first place.

Blade Irons

Until the 1960s, these were the only irons available. The blade is a clean-lined club with a short head, a slender sole and a small sweet spot. Any ball not struck from the middle of the clubface will not fly as it is supposed to. That is why today blades are designed for and played by only the best golfers.

Because of its small dimensions, the blade has more mass behind the sweet spot, channelling your power and control right to where it is needed if you hit the ball from the centre of the clubface every time. Good, traditional golfers believe that blades give them a better feedback, mainly because they are forged from mild steel, and that they are better suited for finesse shots.

Most blades have a large amount of weight in the bottom of the clubhead to lower the centre of gravity. This allows the golfer to hit a higher ball so that it lands more softly. But a few clubmakers produce models which have less weight around the sole, allowing the player to hit a lower shot in areas with a lot of wind.

Obviously, with such a small clubhead, there is a limit to what clubmakers can do about weight distribution. And while I like the looks of the classic blades and have designed quite a few myself for professionals, low handicappers, and traditionalists, I believe that with the advancement of modern technology in clubhead design,

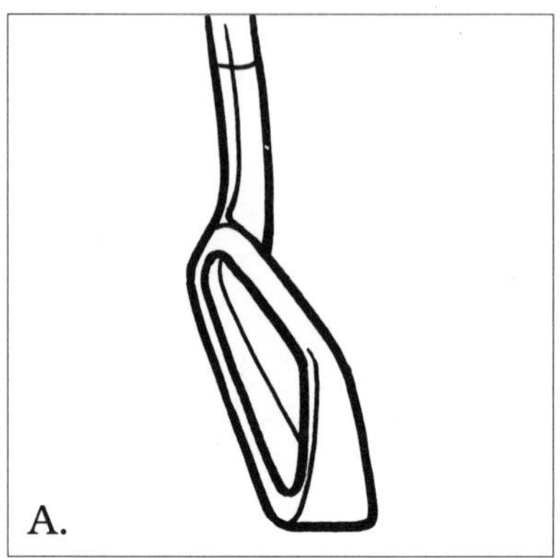

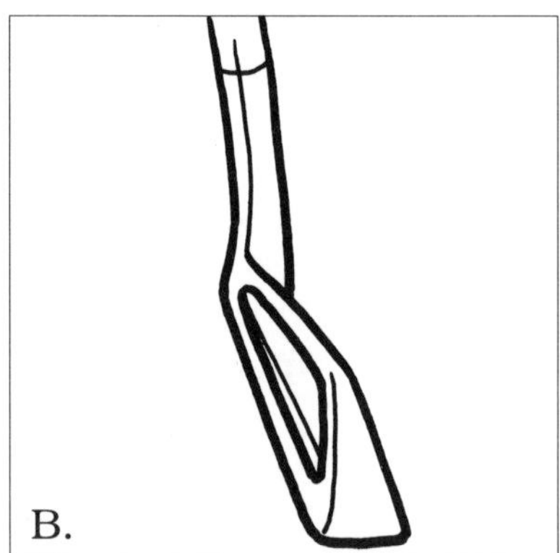

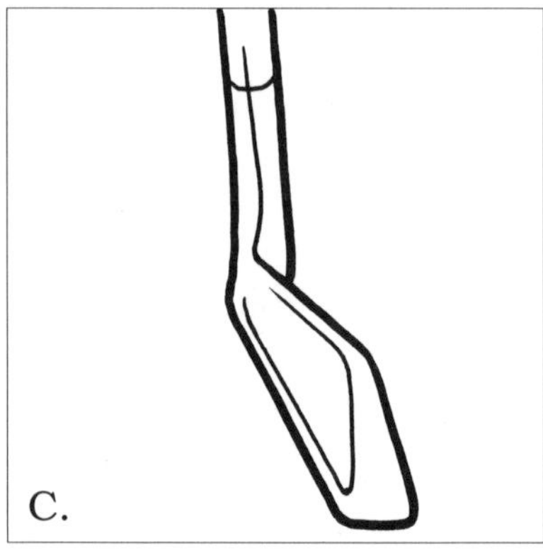

A. Most oversized perimeter-weighted irons have a cavity back. B. The perimeter-weighted semi-blade is smaller and slimmer. C. The traditional blade is the most elegant iron with a tiny sweet spot.

especially in the past decade, the days of the blades are numbered.

Oversized Perimeter-Weighted Irons

These clubs range at the opposite side of the spectrum. Their prototype emerged from the factories about thirty years ago with the weight distributed between heel and toe. While these clubs were designed to improve the accuracy and distance of mis-hit shots, they also tended to have undesired side effects. With too much weight at either end the clubs were likely to open or close depending on the golfer's swing, aggravating the mistakes.

As designs were improved upon, the clubhead grew bigger, and the weight was distributed more evenly around the edges to increase the hitting area and expand the sweet spot. Perimeter-weighted irons, cast in stainless steel or alloys, generally have a wide sole and a cavity at the back. These game-improvement characteristics give better results for off-centre shots allowing the average golfer to make the most out of his or her playing abilities. They also tend to instill more confidence in the golfer through their sheer size.

The Ping Eye-2, the world's best-selling club is a prime example of the oversized perimeter-weighteds. Although originally designed for the amateur, this club is widely used on the pro circuit and was played to victory in major championships on four occasions. Some manufacturers are moving to even bigger clubheads, but now most of the new irons are mid-sized.

Perimeter-Weighted Semi-Blade Irons

Clubs like MacGregor's Jack Nicklaus Personal, Hogan's Edge or the Daiwa Advisor Cavity Back are among the latest designs, made especially for the mid handicapper by offering the best of both worlds: the game-improvement advantages of the perimeter-weighted clubs and the sleek look and feel of the blade. Semi-blades have a slightly longer clubhead than blades, but are forged from mild steel like blades, hence the same feel.

Mix and Match

It's common these days to see tournament professionals who use traditional blades having a perimeter-weighted, offset 1-iron in their bags. Even for a pro, the 1-iron is a hard club to hit and so many take advantage of what technology has to offer.

Taking the principle of perimeter-weighting a step further, some companies offer two types of clubs, blades and perimeter-weighteds, in one set. Cleveland Classics sell traditional blades and semi-blades which have the same dimensions except the semi-blade is perimeter-weighted and you can mix the two. The common choice is perimeter-weighted long and mid irons and blade short irons. Added to this is a wide range of wedges to choose from.

Taylor Made introduced the ICW 11 blades which look the same throughout the set but the 1-iron to 5-iron heads are hollow in the middle to give the effect of perimeter-weighting while the 6-iron through to the wedge are regular blades.

Loft

Quite a few amateurs and even professionals are cavalier about lofts, the degree a clubface is angled in relation to the sole. The more loft, the more backspin is imparted on the ball at impact, and the higher its trajectory, and vice versa.

You can customize the loft in your clubs to match your needs. If you hit the ball high, you need less loft. If you hit the ball low, you may require more. As a rule of thumb, lofts should vary from one club to the next in line by about 4°. However, in practice this is not always the case. With some club manufacturers, the loft can vary by plus or minus 2°.

If you have a 7-iron in your bag that you can really hit a mile, and a 6-iron that doesn't seem to move the ball, they may have lofts for 6.5- and 5.5- irons respectively. You can also end up with two different irons of the same set which have identical lofts.

Loft standards between manufacturers also vary quite a bit, which may account for the fact that your playing partner hits his irons ten yards farther than you. It could just be that his 4-iron has the loft of your 3-iron.

Your professional probably has a loft-and-lie machine, where you can double-check the loft on your clubs to make sure you have the correct loft spacing between clubs.

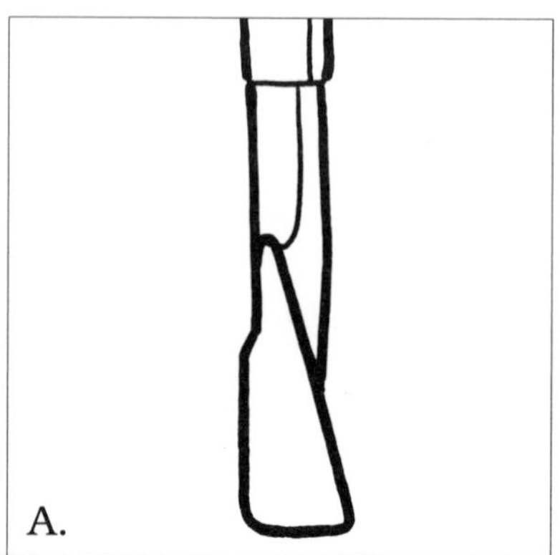

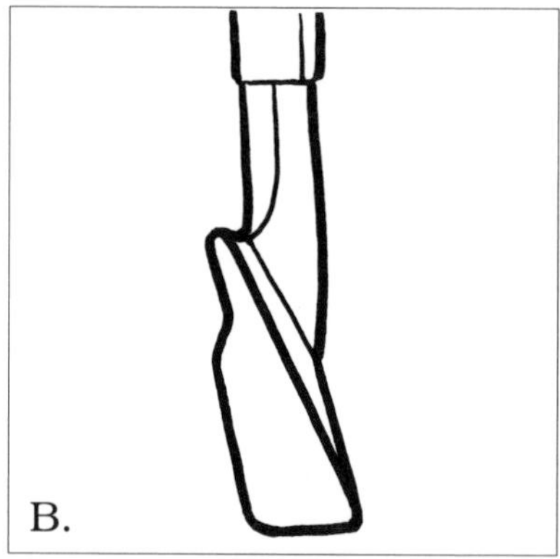

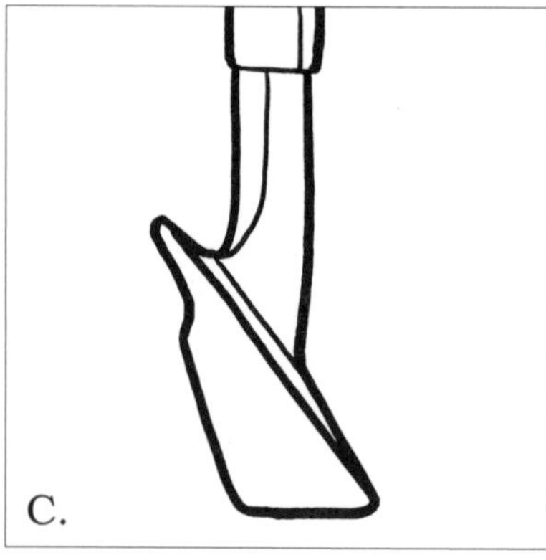

A. The loft of a 1-iron is very slight with about 16° B. The 5-iron shows a much more pronounced loft of 28° C. The clubface of the 9-iron has a loft of 44°

Lie

The lie of a golf club, when it is properly grounded, is of utmost importance in selecting equipment. It is determined by the shape of the clubhead sole, the angle at which the shaft is attached to the clubhead, and the length of the shaft. As a result, the lie affects the plane and the radius of your swing.

The angle between clubhead and shaft is more acute with the upright lie, therefore lifting the toe of the club off the ground. With the flat lie the angle between clubhead and shaft is wider, therefore lifting the heel off the ground.

The more upright the lie, the straigher you hit the ball, because you swing the club on line with the ball longer this way. The flatter the lie, the wider the arc. It can help you to generate more clubhead speed.

However, if the lie is too upright for your stance, you will tend to hook. If the lie is too flat, you will tend to slice. Furthermore, you will tend to dig the toe with a flat lie. So if you want to err, you should err with an upright lie.

Every golfer tries to address the ball properly, even if the lie of the club doesn't suit him or her. Consequently, the player will change his stance to suit the lie of the club. This obviously courts disaster. Instead of changing your stance to suit the lie of the club, you need to change the lie of the club to suit your stance.

A. A player with a flat lie. The heel of the club is off the ground B. This golfer has a club with the correct lie angle. C. The toe of the club is off the ground, this lie is to upright.

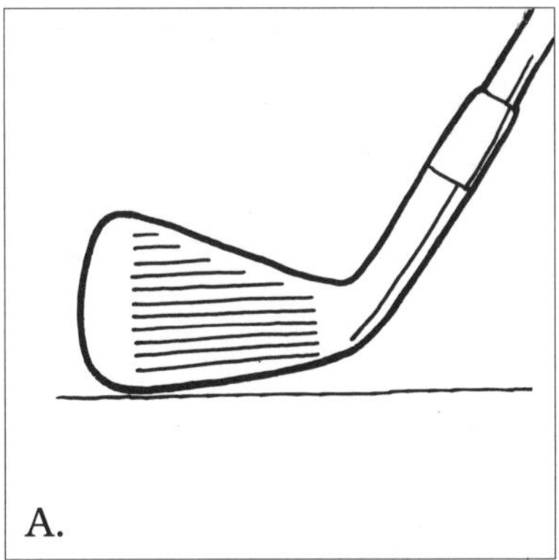

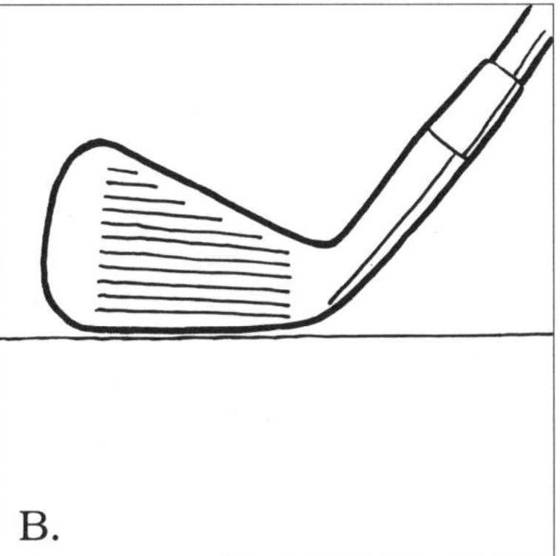

A. The lie of the club is too flat for this player. B. This is what it should look like. C. This lie is too upright for the player.

Average Clubhead Shapes

	1 IRON	2 IRON	3 IRON	4 IRON	5 IRON	6 IRON	7 IRON	8 IRON	9 IRON	PW IRON	SW IRON
LOFT ANGLE	16°	18°	20°	24°	28°	32°	36°	40°	44°	48°	56°
LIE ANGLE	56°	57°	58°	59°	60°	61°	62°	63°	64°	64°	64°
DEAD WEIGHT REGULAR	13.75 oz	14 oz	14.25 oz	14.5 oz	14.75 oz	15 oz	15.25 oz	15.5 oz	15.75 oz	16 oz	16.25 oz
FREQUENCY REGULAR	288 cpm	292 cpm	296 cpm	300 cpm	304 cpm	308 cpm	312 cpm	316 cpm	320 cpm	324 cpm	328 cpm
CLUB LENGTH	39.5″	39″	38.5″	38″	37.5″	37″	36.5″	36″	35.5″	35.5″	35.5″

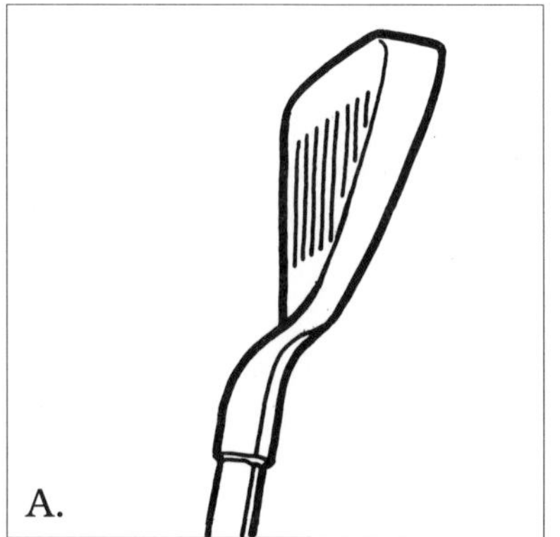

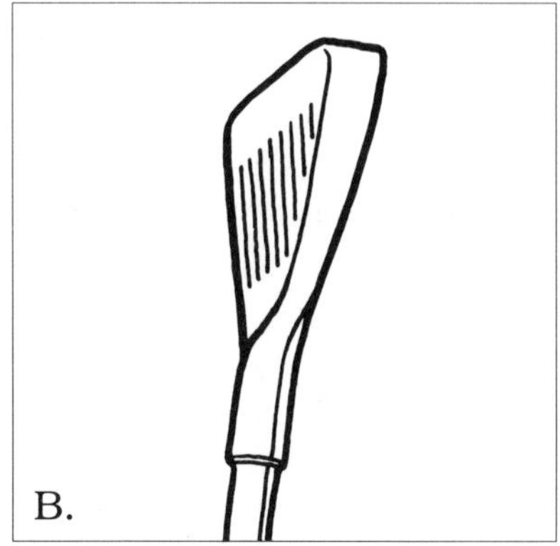

A. The clubhead of the offset club is set behind the shaft to facilitate hand action. It may work for you, but I don't believe that a golfer should play with the hands ahead of the ball.

B. This is how a club without offset looks to the player. Ideally a golfer should have his hands in line with the clubhead, where the traditional clubs put them.

When trying out new equipment, have a close look at the lie of the club. Do you have to move closer to the ball than usual? Do you have to move away? Do you have to shift the club to the left or right to get it properly soled? If your answer to any of the above is yes, the club has the wrong lie for you.

With the correct lie, the long irons and woods should show a slight gap between the toe of the clubhead and the ground at address, as the shaft tends to bring the toes down on the longer, faster swings. You can easily check the lie of the club by grounding it, and having your playing partner slip a piece of paper under the toe. If the paper passes to about the centre of the clubhead with the long clubs, the lie is right for you. The shorter the irons, the smaller the gap. The wedge should sit almost flat on the ground.

Offset

Most perimeter-weighted clubs feature an offset clubhead. You will easily recognize the difference when you compare a blade and a game-improvement club. With a blade iron, the shaft is just about in line with the leading edge which lies between clubface and sole. With an offset, the leading edge of the clubhead is set behind the shaft, creating a lag effect when the player swings the club. The offset club forces the higher handicapper to keep his hands in front of the ball at impact, and assists him in getting his ball airborne.

The reasoning behind offset is simple. The high handicapper may get his hands behind the clubhead at impact, and thus send the ball on a low trajectory.

However, if the clubhead arrives late, it will deal the ball a more steeply descending blow, imparting more backspin on the ball and sending it on a higher trajectory.

Having said that, I personally don't think anybody should play with his hands ahead of the ball. Ideally, your hands should be in line with the clubhead at impact. But if offset clubs look appealing to you, by all means, go ahead.

The latest innovation in clubhead design is the progressive offset, which may vary between 0.39 inches for a 1-iron, 0.25 inches for a 5-iron, and 0.1 inches for a sand wedge. Again, the principle behind it is that the 1-iron with its long shaft and its wide swing arc needs more offset than the wedge with its shorter shaft and steeper angle of downswing.

Although the Tommy Armour 845s, one of the first sets of irons with progressive offset, have been tremendously successful, I strongly recommend that you make sure you get consistent offset througout the set. If you don't, you will have problems hitting all your clubs equally well in the long run. All your clubs, from the 1-iron to the wedge, should show the same angle between the leading edge and the shaft.

Leading Edge

The leading edge of a golf club is where the clubface meets the sole. As such, it plays an important role in the way you ground and play your club, and you want to make sure that you get the kind of leading edge that suits your game.

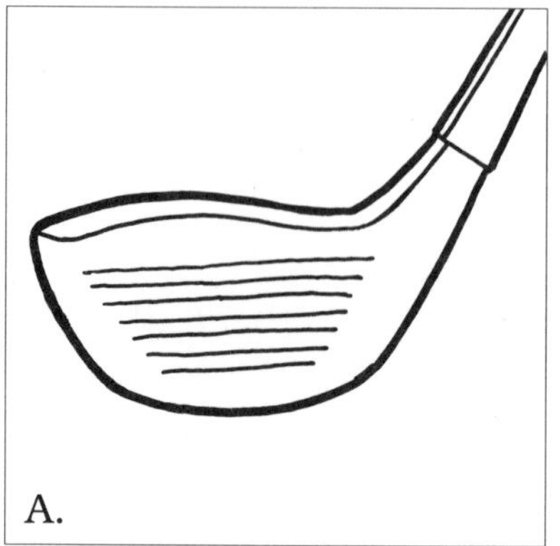

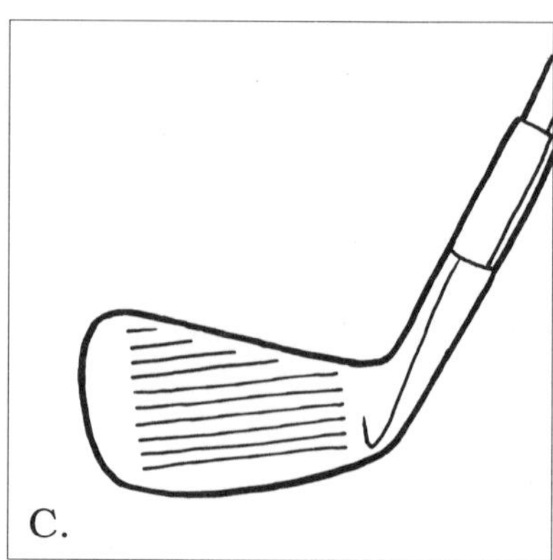

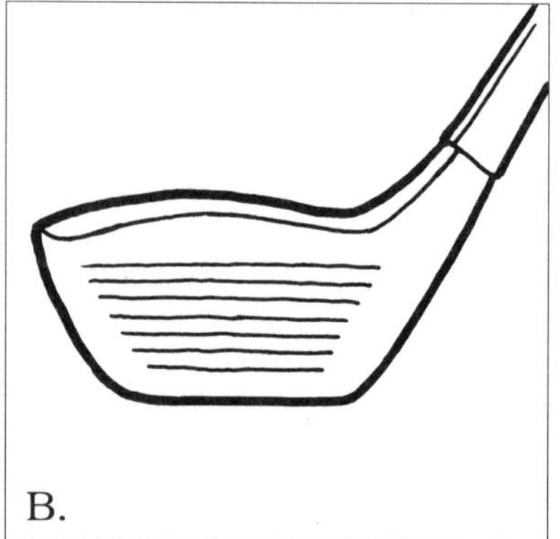

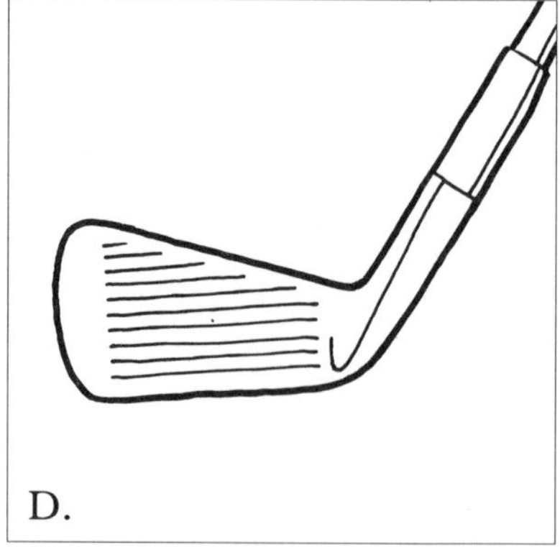

A. The rounded leading edge of the wood may get you off the ground better. B. The straight leading edge is easier to aim.

C. The same round edge on an iron comes with the same advantages and problems. D. The straight edge is preferred by better players.

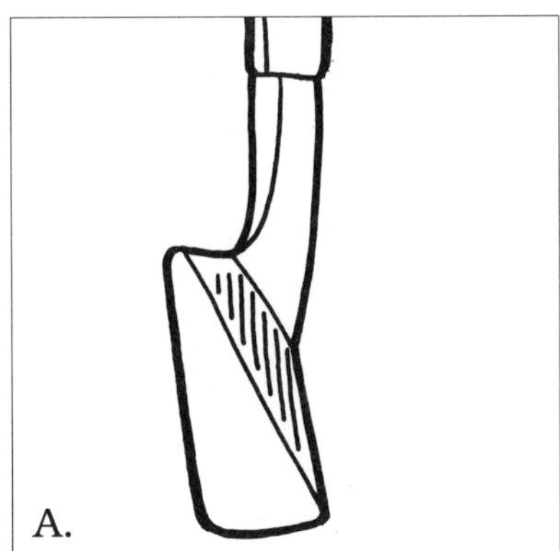

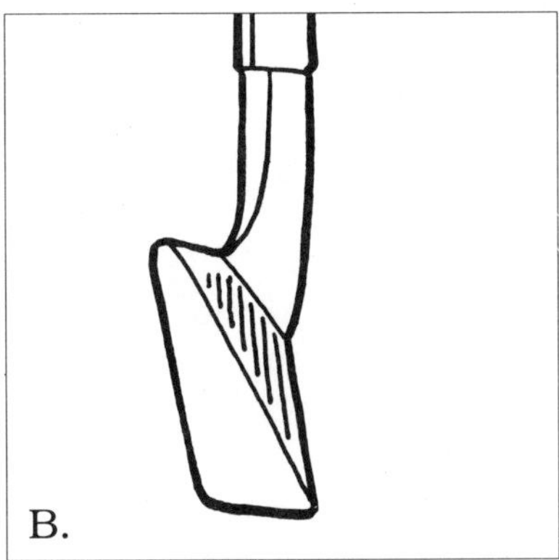

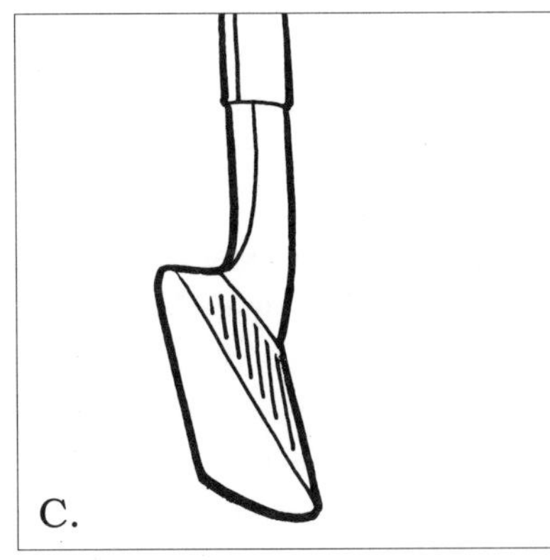

A. This club has bounce. Its leading edge is higher than its trailing edge. B. This club with a straight sole has no bounce. C. This club's leading edge lies lower than its trailing edge. It has negative bounce.

In general, the straighter the leading edge, the straighter you will hit the ball, because it is easier to aim a straight line at the target than a curved one. On the other hand, a curved leading edge makes the club easier to ground and hit, especially off the fairway. You will have noticed that your fairway woods, which are usually more curved than irons, are easier to hit in the rough. The setback is, of course, that they are more difficult to aim.

Bounce

Bounce refers to the relation between the leading edge and the trailing edge of the grounded club, and is determined by the lateral radius of the sole. A cambered sole offers more bounce than a straighter sole. A club with a lower trailing edge and a higher leading edge has bounce. If both edges are level, the club has no bounce. And a club with a higher trailing edge and a lower leading edge has negative bounce.

To determine the amount of bounce you need, you have to analyze the kind of shots you hit. If you hit the ball with a descending blow and take out a good divot every time, you require a club with some bounce to prevent you from digging in too deep. However, if you sweep the ball off the ground, you need less bounce.

Although entire sets of irons are now offered with progressive degrees of bounce ranging from – 3° for the 1-iron through 0° for the 7-iron and 10° for the sand wedge, I personally recommend that you get the same degree of bounce throughout the set with the exception of the sand wedge, which must have more. You should, however, never have negative bounce on your clubs.

Gear Effect

As you look down the face of a fairway wood or driver, you will find that it is slightly bulged from heel to toe. The bulge was introduced to counteract the gear effect, which sends a ball hit at the toe to the left, and a ball hit at the heel to the right, as the ball skids across the clubface after impact. The bulge should bring the ball back to a straighter line of flight.

Not all bulges are created equal. So if you go out to buy new clubs, you have to also take aesthetics into consideration. If you like the look of a bulging clubface, get one. If you prefer the look of a straighter face, buy that one. When you feel comfortable with the look of your club, it probably helps your game more than the bulge or lack of it.

Roll

The clubface also bulges from top to bottom, which is called roll. Again, this kind of bulge is meant to correct an off-centre shot, one that is hit too low or too high. I don't see much advantage in roll.

Grooves

Grooves in clubheads are designed to grip the ball at impact and impart more backspin on it. The width of and distance between grooves and the area of the clubface that may be grooved are regulated by the Rules of Golf.

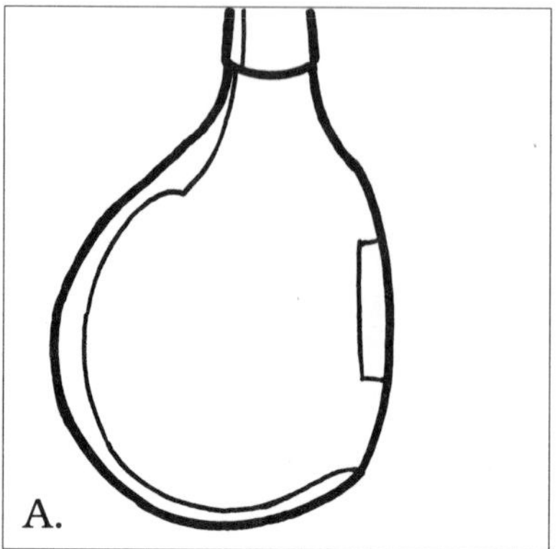

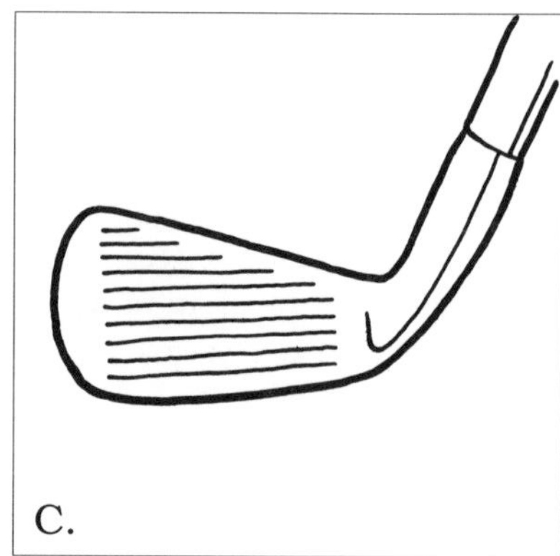

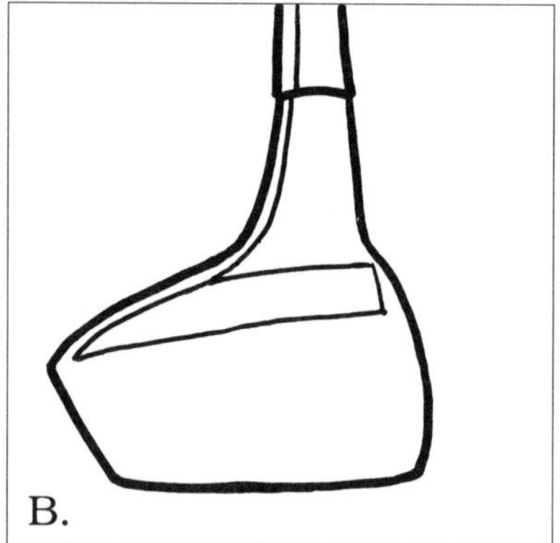

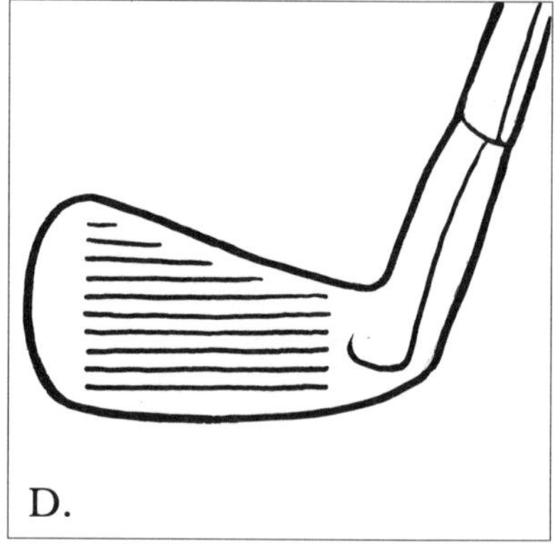

A. A bulging clubface is geared to redirect your mis-hit shots back to the centre. B. Roll does the same for too high or too low shots.

C. The overslung hosel is bent towards the toe to shift the centre of gravity more towards the centre of the club. D. The underslung hosel is bent towards the player and has the centre of gravity closer to the heel.

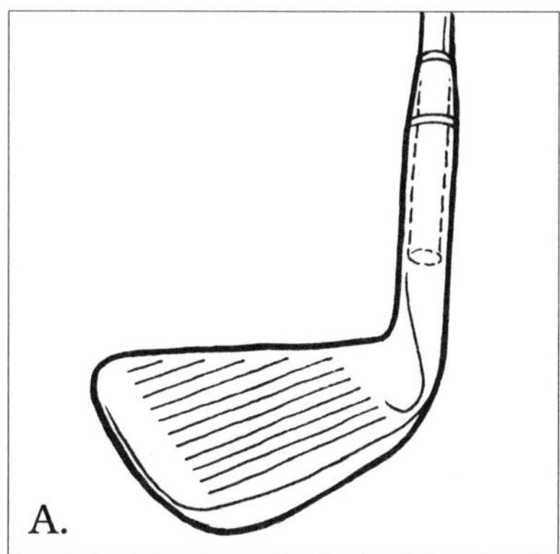

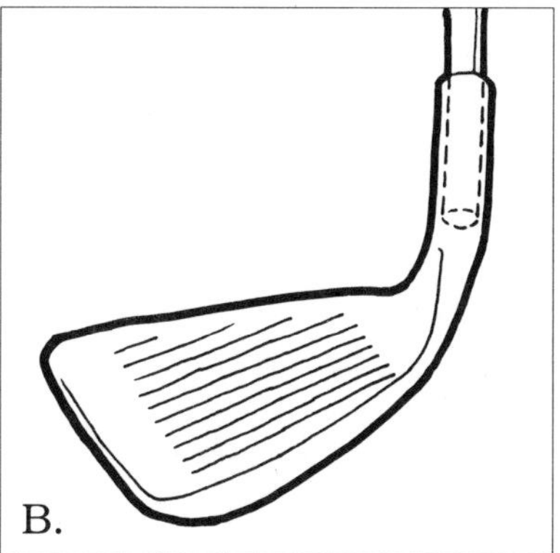

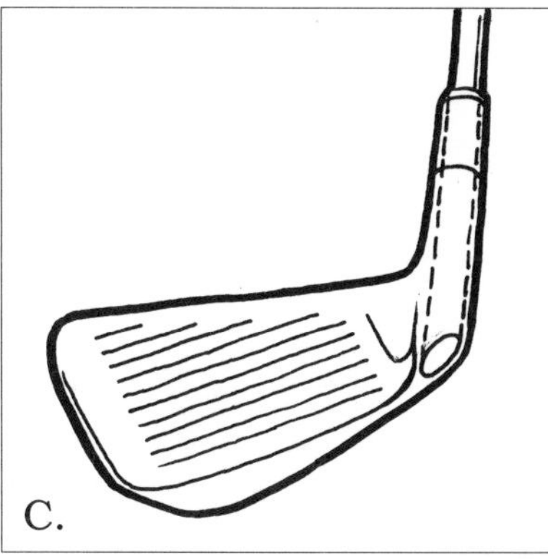

A. The joint here is a conventional, solid connection with weight accumulation around the heel. B. A simpler joint has a shorter part of the shaft inserted into the hosel. C. The new bore-through shaft, which penetrates the sole of the clubhead.

And while there may or may not be any advantages for different shapes of grooves, a roughened clubface may be of more importance. A recent test appears to have proven that a roughened clubface without grooves imparts more backspin than a smooth clubface with grooves.

Joints

There are several different methods of fitting shafts to clubheads. Usually the shaft is inserted for 1.25 to 1.5 inches into the hosel of the clubhead. The joint obviously accounts for a sizeable amount of weight in the hosel, which manufacturers tried to divert away from the heel through different hosel shapes.

More recently, companies like Callaway have begun to replace the hosel with a bore-through joint in drivers and fairway woods, in which the shaft is inserted right into the clubhead and continues all the way to the sole to give players more direct control over the clubhead. Whether or not this approach works for you is something you will have to find out for yourself, but the weight near the heel of the clubhead has definitely decreased considerably. However, bore-through irons with hosels accumulate more weight around the heel.

Hosel

As we have seen, the centre of gravity is an important feature in clubs, as this is where you hit the ball most efficiently. A good golfer will pay attention to the hosel of his or her irons for that reason.

If clubs are not perimeter-weighted, their centre of gravity will lie close to the heel or shaft of the club. To shift the centre of gravity more towards the centre of the club, efficient irons are fitted with an overslung hosel, one that is bent towards the toe. Good players prefer underslung hosels which are bent towards the player and have the centre of gravity even closer to the heel.

Good players prefer underslung hosels which are bent towards the player and have their centre of gravity even closer to the heel.

The High Handicapper

What you need is a club which, in golf jargon, allows you to get a good piece of the ball. In other words, you need one of the game-improvement clubs, the perimeter-weighted irons and woods. Oversized clubheads should give you the greatest advantage. The larger hitting area should boost your confidence and that is a crucial ingredient for any golfer.

The Mid Handicapper

Because of your greater ability you have a wider choice but it should be confined to the oversized perimeter-weighteds and the semi-blades. You may want to mix-and-match with blade short irons and wedges. The oversized driver is probably suited to your ability.

The Low Handicapper

You have the widest choice and really it comes down to what you are comfortable with. If you play off a low single-figure handicap then you might like the feel of blades although I would suggest perimeter-weighted long-irons could provide a real advantage with shots to those long par three's and par four's. Because of your ability, you are less inclined to get a huge advantage out of oversized drivers but even some tour pros use them so don't reject the idea.

A Word of Warning

Whenever you purchase new clubs, take your time to get comfortable with them. I haven't met a golfer yet who doesn't get a buzz out of playing with new clubs but you shouldn't expect to blitz the course on your first outing. Practise with your new clubs and remember to pay attention to maintaining good swing fundamentals. In particular, be prepared to take a little longer to get used to your short irons as its harder to key in that feel for distance.

CLUBHEAD MATERIALS

Golf equipment comes in a bewildering array of shapes and materials providing golfers of all abilities with the club that is right for them, while making selection increasingly difficult. The quest for more distance off the tee in particular has led manufacturers to experiment with new materials for clubheads, although classic woods are still used today.

Among the most popular woods are those now made of steel. Graphite is increasingly being used, titanium has emerged and there are even some ceramic- and plastic-headed woods about.

With these new materials comes a variety of clubhead designs because, as opposed to wood, weight distribution can be varied enormously.

If you are in the market for new clubs, you should keep an open mind. While the lure of new-age materials is tempting indeed it may well be that a traditional wood is right for you. The overall compatibility of clubhead, shaft and grip is the key to choosing a good club. First and foremost you must feel comfortable with the clubs you are considering so that you can swing them confidently. It's no good having a club with which you get more distance but which doesn't feel right and has you easing off your shots in order to maintain accuracy.

The following clubhead materials are on offer today in fairway wood and iron design.

Wood

When the first clubmakers began, the only way to manufacture a long-distance club with enough mass in the head was to use wood which was plentiful and could be crafted.

Until the 1970s, woods still deserved their name. Designs were rather traditional, and the only choice you had then was between clubheads carved from a single block of wood and laminated ones.

The solid clubhead, made of persimmon wood, was and is the preferred choice, because it is considered to offer better feel. Since it is also expensive, persimmon is used to manufacture better quality woods.

Laminated maple wood is still used by some manufacturers, and is in fact very effective. Don't think a laminated clubhead is necessarily inferior. If the club is well made and fitted with a top-quality shaft, there is no reason why it shouldn't work.

If you like the feel of wooden heads, stick with them. Many successful tour players, including Nick Faldo, Fred Couples and Ian Woosnam tried metal-headed drivers but have since gone back to persimmon.

Wooden heads in general tend to suit the better golfer, because wood cannot offer the game-improvement characteristics that metal or composite heads do.

It is very difficult for a layman today to tell the difference between a good and a bad wooden clubhead. Ideally, good wood should have a rather dense grain and be of a dark brown colour, indicating that the wood has matured and won't warp any more. However, woods may be stained or treated with a dark veneer, making a sound judgement almost impossible.

It is of utmost importance that you protect your wooden clubheads well from shocks and moisture. You must wipe them after every shot when playing in wet conditions and dry them in an airy room, but not near a radiator. If you take care of them well, wooden clubs age gracefully.

Metal

When metal-headed woods were first released in the 1970s, they failed to grab the public's imagination, mainly because the heads were quite small and golfers still wanted a large hitting area. Clubmakers overcame that problem with innovative weight distribution which allowed metal-headed woods to be designed along the lines of conventional wooden heads.

The next breakthrough came with the refinement of lightweight graphite shafts which complemented metal heads, and now metal drivers and fairway woods dominate the market with a mind-boggling range of products.

Metal woods offer two distinct advantages over wooden clubs: they can be perimeter-weighted, which helps to correct mis-hit shots, and their weight can be customized for steel, graphite or titanium shafts. The light metal woods allow you to gain clubhead speed and therefore distance.

Through the 1980s, metal-headed woods were refined. Oversized and midsized heads, low profile heads and heads without necks are all designed for a particular purpose whether it be lowering the centre of gravity, reducing twist or increasing the hitting area. Metal woods also come in a great variety of lofts.

Error-correcting metal woods with hooded or open faces, usually about 2° either way, as well as square ones are designed for the golfer who has an ingrained swing fault, such as a slice, but who does not have the time or inclination to go to the practice fairway and correct the problem.

The disadvantage of metal heads is the loss of feel in comparison to wooden clubs. But since the Rules of Golf changed in January, 1992 to allow inserts, the faces of some metal-headed woods and irons are fitted with graphite inserts to give a softer feel at impact.

Graphite

Clubmakers are now manufacturing graphite-headed woods which offer many of the advantages of metal heads, but are mainly found among oversized drivers and lightweight clubs. The combination of a lightweight shaft and a graphite head allows the golfer to produce maximum clubhead speed with little effort as the ball bounces back from the more springy graphite head at impact like an athlete on a trampoline.

A common problem, however, is a loss of feel for the club during the swing, which manufacturers tried to overcome by increasing the size of the clubhead.

The weight difference between an all-graphite club and others can be as much as three ounces. The latest innovation has been the one-piece graphite with head and shaft combined. There are only a few models about and it is yet to be seen if they will be successful. The principle behind the design is to produce more consistent performance by not having any joints.

For the average golfer, the major disadvantage of graphite-headed clubs is the top-end-of-the-market price. A cheaper alternative may be metal.

Titanium

Titanium shafts have been around for quite some time but titanium heads are a recent innovation. Like graphite, titanium is becoming a popular material in the manufacture of oversized drivers. It has the strength of steel but is far lighter and the size of the clubhead can be expanded more, providing more hitting area.

Also, like graphite, titanium is designed to allow the player to achieve greater clubhead speed – and, like graphite, it is an expensive item.

Plastic

In the 1980s, a few companies experimented unsuccessfully with hi-tech plastics in clubhead design. Even Cobra's range of Ultramid woods, made from bullet-proof plastic, was destined for the scrap heap until John Daly, the longest hitter on the U.S. Tour, won the 1991 PGA Championship using an Ultramid driver.

Daly had chosen the Ultramid out of necessity. He had bent the face of metal-headed drivers and cracked the inlays in traditional wooden models. After his PGA victory, Cobra received 2,000 orders within the next week, the Ultramid remained, and now Cobra has used plastic in the manufacture of other clubs.

The principle behind using plastic is much the same as for using metal. Clubs made of this hard material are designed to generate more power and versatility of design. Obviously, very few people will be able to hit the ball hard enough to damage their equipment but that doesn't mean plastic-headed woods will not be right for them.

Ceramic

Ceramic-headed woods have only been manufactured by a couple of clubmakers and as yet, there has not been any great interest. But as more and more golf shoes are fitted with ceramic-tipped spikes which last longer than others, golfers' awareness of this material will increase.

The perception among golfers, I imagine, is that ceramic is a brittle substance which would not stand up to the pressure of hitting golf balls. In fact, it is one of the harder substances and is even used in the manufacture of automobile engines.

Irons

When you buy a set of irons, you look for clubs which offer playability – you want consistency and control. The lesser need for lightweight irons makes new clubhead materials, for instance the expensive, grahite woven heads, a rare choice. By far the most popular material for irons is steel.

Stainless steel, which is cast, dominates the world markets with perimeter-weighted heads, the overwhelming choice of the average player.

Carbon steel, better known as mild steel, which is forged, is predominantly used for blades, popular with above average amateurs and professionals in all countries. They prefer mild steel because of the softer contact it provides. The ball actually stays on the clubface fractionally longer at impact and comes off softer, giving the player better feel and control, particularly with finesse shots.

A number of companies are now producing perimeter-weighted clubs in mild steel, because a growing number of better golfers are switching over to game-improvement models, although mild steel is not rust resistant and must be chromed, meaning it does not have as long a life as the harder stainless steel. It's a trade-off between a club that lasts and one that offers better feel.

There have been other materials used, such as beryllium-copper and manganese-bronze, soft alloys which can be dye cast. These were used in the first mild-metal perimeter-weighted clubs but are becoming increasingly rare because of their lack of durability.

Feel

In golf, feel and touch have different meanings. Feel refers mostly to feedback while touch refers to the golfer's ability to control a shot – the level of finesse. Feel contributes to touch. The better feel or feedback a club provides, the more touch the player will have.

Those people who prefer wood to metal-headed woods argue that a *click* at impact is better than a *clang*. Wood provides better feedback, you know instantly whether you've made good contact or not.

The introduction of graphite inserts in the face of metal-headed woods is designed to offer the best of both worlds, the soft feel, similar to wood, with the weight distribution advantages of metal.

You can draw the same comparisons between mild-steel and soft-alloy irons and the harder stainless steel models, although the difference is less noticeable.

How to Choose?

Because of the variety of golfers in the world and the vast range of clubs available, there is no strict guideline as to what clubhead material you should choose, so I will offer some broad classifications.

The Novice Golfer

You should still have your clubs made to measure where possible, but don't spend too much. Your swing will change through coaching or simply by playing often, and your level of competence will most likely outgrow your first set of clubs before they are worn out. There's no reason to spend large amounts of money on clubs you may use for only one year. What you should look at are steel and wood, the materials used in the budget-priced clubs.

The High Handicapper

Your best bet is probably a game-improving, perimeter-weighted stainless steel headed club. It will last longer than mild steel, and is available in greater range of models.

If you have a big budget and are looking for more distance, graphite may work for you. Virtually every graphite-headed wood or iron is light and designed for the average golfer. The same applies for titanium, although few titanium irons are available.

The Mid Handicapper

You may want something that offers better feel, particularly in the range of specialty wedges. Mild steel and soft alloy game-improvement semi-blades which are moderately perimeter-weighted, may be the answer. In general, however, the materials that suit the high handicapper will suit you as well.

The Low Handicapper

You can play a greater variety of shots, and are looking for the type of club which does the job best. This may lead to a great deal of mix-and-match in your bag. A good golfer's choice may comprise a metal-headed driver with graphite shaft, a persimmon-headed wood with steel shaft, perimeter-weighted stainless steel-headed 1-iron of one brand and mild steel blades of another.

2599431.

SHAFTS

The greatest misgiving I have when golfers select equipment is that they will look at what type of clubhead they prefer, but rarely do they look at the shaft as the most important component.

I doubt more than one or two percent of the world's golfing population is playing with the right shafts. You can take the best clubhead made, fit it with the wrong shaft, and, try as you might, you won't be able to hit the ball consistently well. Shaft specifications are vital to touring professionals who are more able to compensate, through their ability, for the inadequacies of a piece of equipment, so it is immeasurably more important for the average golfer to have his or her clubs set up the right way.

Steel

The overwhelming choice for shafts is steel which has been around since hickory began to be phased out in the 1920s. Hickory was still used by some golfers through the thirties but by the forties just about everyone had changed to steel. Steel shafts are available in many flexes, with various kick points, and also in regular and light weights. Steel is the cheapest material for shafts, and because of its high level of performance, golfers see little need to change, particularly with irons.

Graphite

Graphite shafts, which are sometimes also called composite, boron-graphite or carbon-fibre shafts, are light shafts designed to lower the overall weight of the club making it easier to create more clubhead speed, and thus propel the ball farther.

As golfers look for maximum distance off the tee, graphite shafts are today more frequently used for fairway woods and especially metal-headed drivers than for irons. Although the quality control for graphite is now very good, and the same range of flexes and kick points are available as for steel shafts, prices are still high, and may prevent golfers from switching.

Titanium

The development of titanium shafts has also advanced but not to the degree of refinement achieved with graphite. The range of specifications for titanium shafts is limited because of their construction. With no steps, as there are in steel shafts, kick point regulation is limited and the torque level is related directly to the diameter of the shaft and width of the shaft wall, as opposed to graphite where different strain carbon fibres are used. The major advantage is that titanium has the strength of steel but is lighter, hence a lightweight shaft. The major disadvantage is, again, the price.

Flex

The most important characteristic of the shaft is flex; you must chose the right amount of flex for your needs. Here are a few rules to consider. The stiffer the shaft, the straighter the ball flies. The more flexible the shaft, the farther it flies. However, if you are not strong enough to generate a high clubhead speed, you will loose distance with a stiff shaft. And if you do generate a high speed clubhead speed, you may hit all over the place with a whippy shaft.

Most men tend to overestimate their strength, and buy stiffer shafts than they need. If you are overswinging to get distance, it's a sure sign the shafts in your clubs are too stiff. The right amount of flex will allow you to make solid contact and achieve maximum distance with a controlled swing. So do yourself a favor and don't take your ego into the pro shop.

Borrow sample clubs with different shaft flexes. You will find that you tend to slice a ball with a club that is too stiff for you, because it requires more clubhead speed to square the face at impact. A shaft that is too whippy for you on the other hand may lead to a hook. If you find a shaft with which you can hit a mid iron straight, you are on to something. Find out how you fare with distance versus accuracy for the rest of the set.

The two major manufacturers of steel shafts, True Temper and Apollo, offer an enormous range of flexes. To give you some idea, Apollo's Masterflex comes in regular, firm, stiff, tourstiff and extrastiff flexes and that is just one of eleven models of steel shafts they have, which include women's shafts and another range for senior golfers. True Temper offers five steel shaft models and overall makes more than 30 flexes.

Although most players have shafts of the same flex fitted to every club in their bag, you may want more flex for your pitching wedge and sand wedge.

This will allow you to throttle back on the shots that require more finesse. If you are an experienced player, you may start a mix-and-match of flexes according to your needs.

Kick Point

Another recent innovation in shaft design is the positioning of the kick point or flex point, that part of the shaft which bends the most during the swing. Shafts are now made with either a high, mid or low kick point. Ideally, the kick point should complement the flex of the shaft providing a more refined shaft for the golfer.

As with flex, the choice of the right kick point amounts to a choice between length and accuracy. The lower the kickpoint, the more length you gain, and the more accuracy you sacrifice. The higher the kick point, the more accuracy you gain, and the more length you sacrifice.

Generally, stronger players prefer high kick points to avoid additional vibration near the clubhead, while weaker players need a low kickpoint to generate more clubhead speed. But strength is not the only

A.

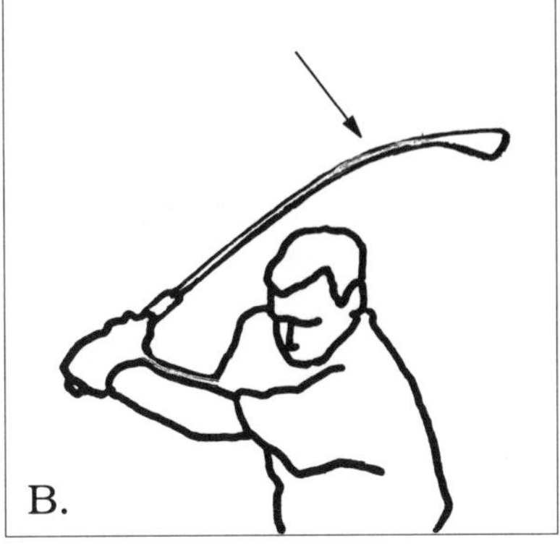
B.

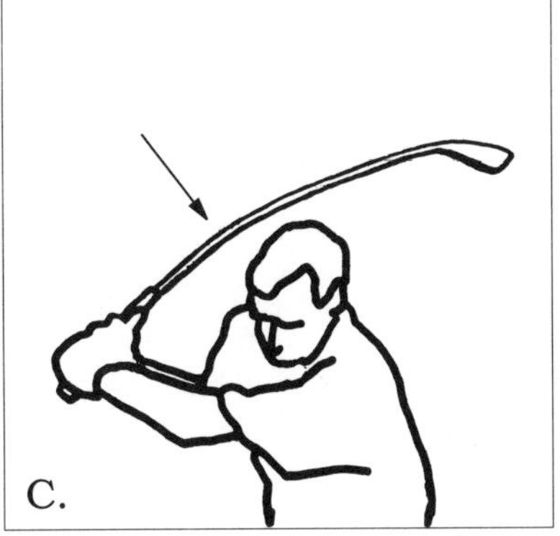
C.

A. A mid kick point suits mid handicappers, swingers and weaker hitters. The flexibility of the club is highest at its middle.

B. A low kick point is preferred by high handicappers and weaker golfers.
C. A high kick point is best for low handicappers and powerful players.

consideration which determines what kick point is right for you, your style of swing is equally important.
If you are a hitter, you hit the ball with a delayed release, and quick hands at impact. That places the shaft under a great amount of stress right before, during, and right after impact. The hitter therefore needs a shaft with more resistence at the bottom, and should opt for a high kick point.

If you are a swinger, you swing with a full body and shoulder turn, and quiet hands at impact. The swinger builds up clubhead speed throughout the downswing, applying stress more evenly along the shaft. You should opt for a lower kickpoint.

A general guideline would look like this:

	Hitter	**Swinger**
Strong	high kick point	mid kick point
Weak	mid kick point	low kick point

Torque

One of the buzzwords in golf these days is torque, which refers to the twist of a shaft under stress. When steel shafts were all you fitted to your clubs, torque was irrelevant for steel shafts have about 2° of twist, but with the growing popularity of graphite shafts, torque has become an integral part of design.

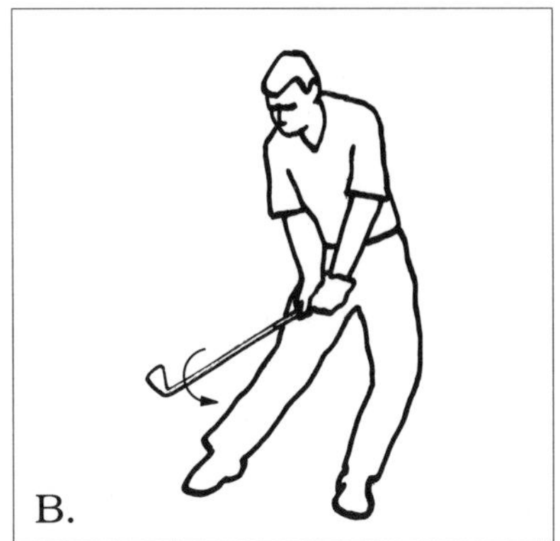

A. The shaft begins to flex at the start of the downswing as pressure is applied along the length of the shaft.

B. The hands rotate through the hitting area as if cracking a whip - the unhinged wrists release the shaft from its flexed position and square the clubhead, creating torque.

Torque runs perpendicular to flex and reacts independently. The shaft flexes as a result of pressure being applied during the downswing. Torque differs in that it is the result of your hands rotating through impact. Think of a golf club as a high speed pendulum, the backswing and follow-through travelling precisely along the target line. The pressure applied during the downswing makes the shaft flex, but without rotation of the clubhead the shaft cannot twist.

Each and every shaft has some degree of torque. It would be beyond the capability of human beings to handle a shaft with no torque at all, as it would have to be extremely stiff.

The ideal degree of torque allows the golfer to return the clubhead to a square position at impact. Too much torque, and the clubhead will close at impact, producing a hook. Not enough torque, and the clubhead stays open, producing a slice.

As for the choice of the right kick point, the correct amount of torque depends on the style of swing, because the golf swing consists of a rotational release through impact. The quicker the rotation the greater the resistance to torque required. This is a rule of thumb for your requirements:

	Hitter	**Swinger**
Strong	low torque	mid torque
Weak	mid torque	high torque

When manufacturers first produced graphite shafts in the 1970s, the control of the torque was their biggest problem. Some added the metal element boron in form of particles or fibres to their shafts. Others used different strain carbon fibres to regulate the torque level. On those shafts you will find the specification high strain or HM (high modulus) with an accompanying number ranging from 30 to 70. The higher the number, the greater the resistance to distortion. The thickness of the shaft wall and its diameter also influence the torque level of the club.

Since the late 1980s, graphite shafts could be constructed with a lower level of torque than steel shafts have, and the production became customized to suit all kinds of golfers. US manufacturer Aldila for example offers shafts with torque ranging from 2° for tour players to 7° for women, seniors and juniors.

Frequency-Matching

This term refers to the even vibration of each club in your set, to ensure that all your shafts react in the same way, which should add consistency to your game.

Frequency-matching is measured in cycles per minute. Because of the different shaft lengths in one set of irons, the frequency varies from club to club by four cycles per minute, if they are properly matched. If you persistently hook or slice with particular clubs from your set, they may not be frequency-matched. Reshafting them can easily solve your problem.

Weight

After the golfer has considered material, flex, kick point and torque, he or she must then look at the weight of the shaft for this has a bearing on the club's overall playing characteristics.

For instance an average, regular Apollo steel shaft with mid kick point weighs about 5.19 ounces, while its exact match in graphite weighs only 4.19 ounces. A light boron-graphite shaft comes to about 3.2 ounces, but without the boron it can weigh as little as 2.6 ounces.

A light shaft will allow the golfer to achieve greater club head speed which, combined with the clubhead having a greater percentage of the club's overall weight, places the shaft under additional stress and it will flex and torque more. This means a stiffer flex is required to give the same playing characteristics as a club with a regular-weighted shaft.

A heavier shaft has the reverse effect. A lower percentage of the club's weight is in the clubhead, reducing the amount of stress placed on the shaft; as a result you need a shaft with more flex.

Swing Weight

Simply put, swing weight reflects the weight distribution within a club. The higher the swing weight of a club, the heavier the clubhead in relation to shaft and grip.

SWING WEIGHTS	WOODS	IRONS
B5	17.50 oz	17.83 oz
B6	17.67 oz	18.00 oz
B7	17.83 oz	18.17 oz
B8	18.00 oz	18.33 oz
B9	18.17 oz	18.50 oz
C0	18.33 oz	18.67 oz
C1	18.50 oz	18.83 oz
C2	18.67 oz	19.00 oz
C3	18.83 oz	19.17 oz
C4	19.00 oz	19.33 oz
C5	19.17 oz	19.50 oz
C6	19.33 oz	19.67 oz
C7	19.50 oz	19.83 oz
C8	19.67 oz	20.00 oz
C9	19.83 oz	20.17 oz
D0	20.00 oz	20.33 oz
D1	20.17 oz	20.50 oz
D2	20.33 oz	20.67 oz
D3	20.50 oz	20.83 oz
D4	20.67 oz	21.00 oz
D5	20.83 oz	21.17 oz
D6	21.00 oz	21.33 oz
D7	21.17 oz	21.50 oz
D8	21.33 oz	21.67 oz
D9	21.50 oz	21.83 oz
E0	21.67 oz	22.00 oz
E1	21.83 oz	22.17 oz
E2	22.00 oz	22.33 oz
E3	22.17 oz	22.50 oz
E4	22.33 oz	22.67 oz
E5	22.50 oz	22.83 oz

The lower the swing weight, the lighter the clubhead in relation to shaft and grip. The dead weight of each of the club's components – clubhead, shaft and grip – determines its swing weight, which has a direct impact on the way a club and its shaft perform.

For example, changing from a regular shaft to a light weight shaft will reduce the dead weight of the club, but increase its swing weight, because a greater percentage of the dead weight is now in the clubhead. If you change any one of the components in your club, the swing weight changes as well.

A lighter swing weight places less stress on the shaft during your swing. If you fit identical shafts to clubs with different swing weights the shaft on the club with a lighter swing weight would perform like a stiffer shaft. Counteracting this phenomenon to a degree is the fact that you should achieve greater clubhead speed with the lighter club. There is, however, no remedy for the loss of feel that accompanies a light swing weight.

Finding the optimum swing weight is a matter of trial and error, but it's vital you go through the trouble to find out what's right for you. Swing weight is available from A_0 to F_9. In golf clubs, it usually ranges from C_6, used by women and juniors, through D_2 for men. Just remember, if you change any of the components of the club, the swing weight changes as well.

The Short Hitter

You need a shaft with zip. Whether steel, graphite or titanium, the shaft should have a generous amount of flex so that you can achieve maximum power with a comfortable, controlled swing. A low kick point will help you hit the ball with a higher trajectory while the level of torque in graphite shafts should be around 7°.

The Average Hitter

You don't want a shaft with too much flex or torque or you will have trouble maintaining control. But then you don't want to overestimate your strength. You want a club with regular flex and mid-range torque, around 4° or 5°, if you are fitting a graphite shaft. Depending on how you swing the club you should consider a mid or low kick point.

The Power Hitter

A stiff shaft will give you the best control over your shots. If you like regular shafts you need to be swinging the club well to maintain control. Stiff flex is the safest choice. Depending on how you swing the club, a high or mid kick point is preferable although stiff shafts are also made with low kick points. The level of torque you require would probably range from 2° to 3.5°.

GRIPS

In golf, it is often the detail that counts and grips are no exception. Jack Nicklaus told me once that his club manufacturer couldn't produce another set that felt the same as the one he was using. After pulling a couple of his clubs apart, I found that the problem lay with the grips.

The grips on his original clubs were sealed with a plastic cap, while the newer sets had a rubber cap with a hole in it to let the air escape. The clubs sounded different during the swing, and felt very different as well at impact mainly because the newer cap was made of rubber and not plastic.

Grips are the only link between you and your club. If they don't feel right and don't fit properly into your hand, the club will move during your swing, and you will lose control.

Sizes

It is an absolute necessity to have grips that are neither too thick nor too thin for your hand, or else the finest equipment will fail you.

If your grips are too thick for you, your muscles will tense to hold on to them. This makes it difficult for you to release the club, and may cause a slice. Too thick a grip will definitely impede any intentional draw shot you plan to hit.

If the grip is too thin for your hand, your muscles won't be very tense, allowing you to release easily, maybe too easily and too early for your swing. An early release means your clubface has closed at impact, causing a hook.

Here is a simple way of telling whether the grips on your clubs are right for you. Place your top hand around the grip as you would normally hold your club. If the tip of your middle finger barely touches the thumb pad, the grip is ideal for you. If your middle finger doesn't reach the thumb pad, the grip is too thick for you. If your middle finger pushes into the thumb pad, the grip is too thin for you.

You would also be well advised to double-check if the grips on your existing set are all the same size. Unfortunately, you can't take this for granted. And, obviously, you need to have the same feel for all your clubs and all your grips.

Materials

Once you have found the correct size for your grips, experiment with different grip materials to find the one that you feel the most comfortable with. Quite a few good golfers like the feel of leather grips, and don't mind paying three to four times the price of rubber or synthetic models. The disadvantages of leather are the amount of care they require as they tend to soak up sweat and get dirty easily. If not taken care of properly, they will become slick.

Rubber grips are by far the most popular, with or without cord inserts. While the rubber grip is relatively kind to tender hands, easy to maintain, and long-lasting, the types with cord inserts may be a bit rough if your hands are sensitive.

A new soft synthetic grip, again with or without cord, has been gaining favour with golfers of all levels. It almost resembles leather, but doesn't require as much care.

Styles

There are many styles of grips on the market today, featuring lines, dots, arrows or other intricate patterns. There are even grips with integrated air-cushions to offer better feel. They may be worth a try.

Manufacturers now produce greatly oversized grips for people with very big hands, but also for golfers who suffer from arthritis and have difficulty closing their hands around the grip.

Again, it is advisable, if you have decided on a style you like, to go and hit a few balls with the club. While grips are cheap, it is extremely important for your performance to get the one that is right for you.

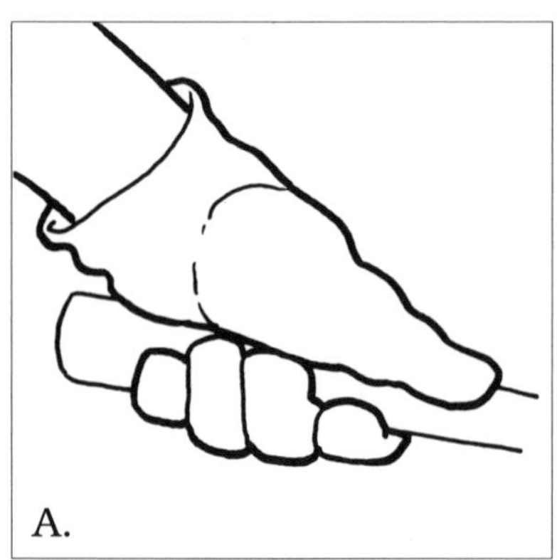
A.

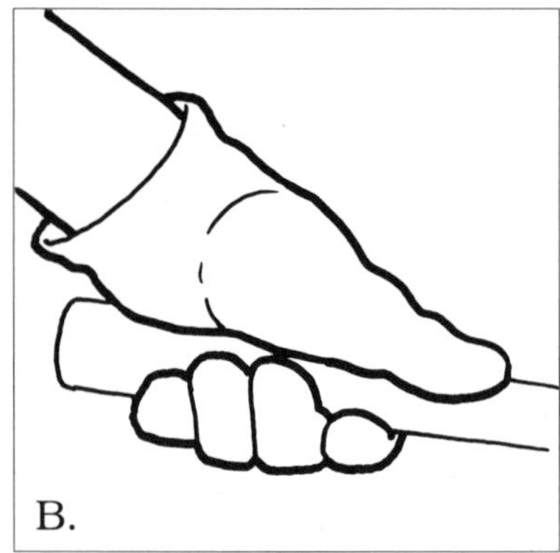
B.

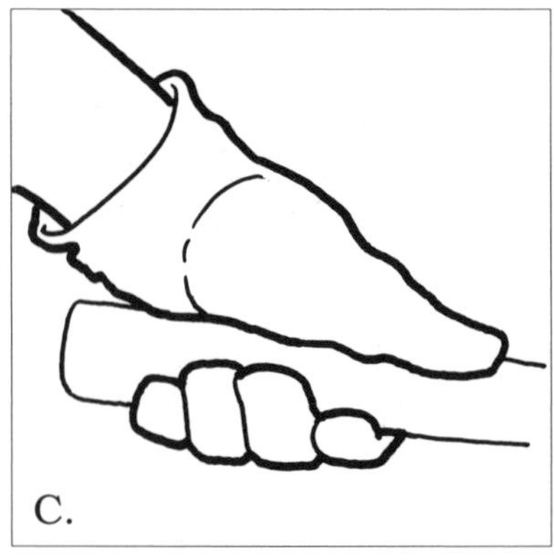
C.

A. The fingers press into the thumb pad. This grip is too thin for the player. B. The middle finger barely touches the hand. This grip is correct. C. There is a gap between fingers and thumb pad. This grip is too thick for the player.

Changing Grips

Once you have found the correct grip size, material and style, your club professional can easily fit new grips to your clubs, even if he doesn't carry stock of different grip sizes, by sticking layers of adhesive tape onto the shaft before pulling the grip over it. This doesn't take more than a few minutes per club.

However, if your new grips have a ridge running down the back of the grip, you must make sure that the ridge runs in a straight line and is positioned right in the centre, because the ridge really tells you where to position your hands. To skirt this problem, quite a number of good golfers prefer grips without ridges.

Another problem you may encounter when your grips are changed is bulging. Check the grips properly after the job has been done, and don't accept poor workmanship. Ask for the grips to be refitted if you aren't satisfied.

Maintenance

As grips are the one and only link to your clubs, they need to be in pristine condition if you want to play your best. You need to clean the grips every three or four rounds of play, to prevent dirt from settling on them for good, making the grip slippery in the short term, and the material hard and brittle in the long term.

You also need to replace the grips on your clubs every three years if you play more than 30 rounds of golf a year. Most golfers neglect to do this, causing the grip to wear where they apply the greatest pressure when holding the club. This in fact makes the grip illegal under the Rules of Golf because such a grip is regarded as a swing aid since it influences the player to grip the club in a certain way — whether rightly or wrongly is irrelevant.

Putter Grips

A putting stroke requires more feel than any other golf shot. Therefore you may want to be especially careful when selecting the putter grip. Most grips are flattened in front to give you a sense of direction when you are stroking the ball. Depending on your individual putting style this may help or distract you. Again, the best method to find the correct grip for your putter is trying out different models.

You may also want to consider excluding putter grips from your usual maintenance routine. A number of professionals believe that a sudden change in the feel of the grip may affect their performance on the green, and thus they don't clean their putter grips.

PUTTERS

Whether simple in design or weird and wonderful, the putter is the club which engenders more feeling than any other in the golfer's bag. The putter can drive you to distraction or be your best friend. Some golfers may use the same putter for thirty years, others may have tried hundreds.

You will have to experiment a lot to find a putter to suit your style. It must instill confidence in you. If you're certain you're going to hole a putt, there's every chance you will.

Materials

A variety of materials ranging from metals, carbon steel, brass, lead, copper and aluminium to modern plastics are used in the manufacture of putter heads. Manganese-bronze and beryllium-copper are heavier than steel and have a softer feel on contact with the ball. As a rule of thumb, heavier putters are preferred on slow greens and lighter putters on fast greens.

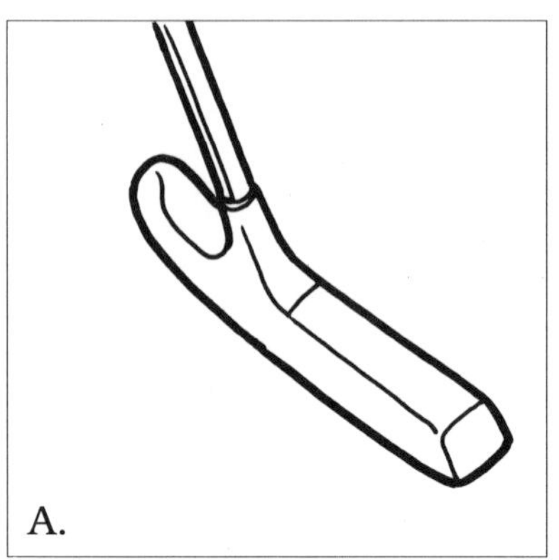

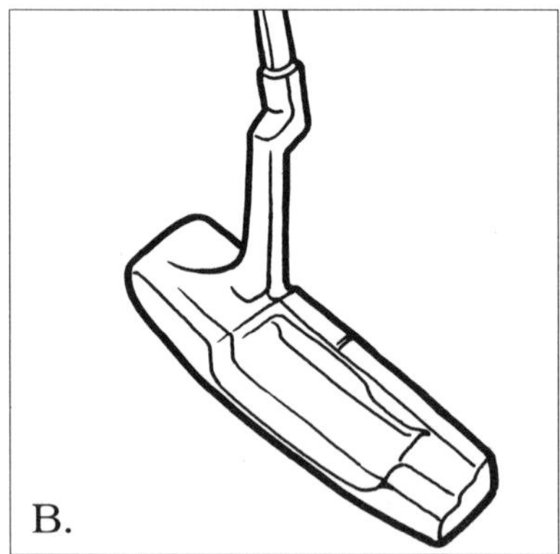

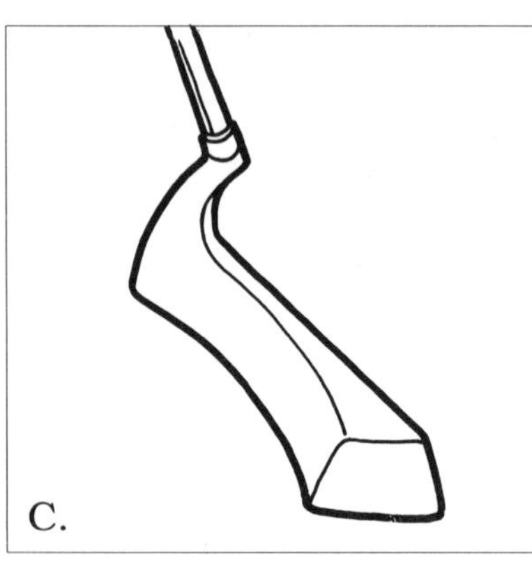

A. The classic blade putter with a straight centre-shaft is an all-time favourite. B. The heel-to-toe weighted putter with a bent neck suits players who put their hands in front of the ball on the green. C. This new putter is designed for golfers who have their hands behind the ball when putting.

Other producers use mild steel and brass for putter heads, both of which have a softer feel than stainless steel, without the added weight of manganese-bronze or beryllium-copper.

The total weight of putters can range from 14 to 23 ounces.

Shapes

While there are thousands of different putters available, there are just three basic head designs: mallet, blade and perimeter-weighted.

Mallets have been used since golf greens were first manicured to provide a reliable putting surface. The mallet is pretty much a smaller version of a wood with the same clubhead shape, but with a shallow face. The first mallets were made from wood before the move to metal. As the long game clubs, mallets have their hosel at the heel. They are still being produced today.

The blade is a simple, clean design. Early models were quite thin, almost like a 1-iron. Some have flanges added to place more weight on the bottom of the blade, assisting you to produce a better pendulum-stroke, which is one of the most effective ways to putt.

Blades either come with the hosel at the heel like Jack Nicklaus' George Low Wizard 600, which the Golden Bear used in all but one of his major championship victories, or with a hosel fitted almost near the centre of the clubhead like the Acushnet Bullseye, which I use.

Perimeter-weighted putters were introduced in the 1960s to balance the clubhead better and to expand the sweet spot. Using these putters will give you a better roll from your off-centre hits. Ping produces about 70 models of these, most of which have offset heads or pronounced goose-neck hosels.

Shafts

While the standard putter lengths vary between 32 and 38 inches, you should choose the one fitting your style of putting best. You may want to have a longer shaft, if you are standing more upright when you putt.

You can even opt for the broomstick putter, which is a perimeter-weighted model with an extra long shaft, designed to take wrist action out of putting. With a broomstick putter, you have to hold the top of the grip close to your chest with one hand, while the other holds the grip where you would hold a conventional putter. The broomstick putter helped a few professionals to overcome the yips, a sort of hiccup in the putting stroke.

While this is something few amateurs ever contemplate, professionals will look at the flex of their putter shafts. There is a trend towards light graphite and titanium shafts, because they give you a better feel for the putter head.

Loft and Lie

Putters need a loft so that the ball gets airborne slightly before it starts to roll. Putters without loft tend to press the ball into the turf and let it skid across the green, making it difficult to hole out.

The standard loft of putters varies between 0° and 5°, averaging around 3°. If you are often playing on longer grass, you may need more loft, or less, if the greens on your home course are particularly smooth.

Another important consideration is the lie you want in your putter, the angle at which the shaft is attached to the clubhead, which can lie anywhere between 66° and 79°. Do you want it flat, so that you position the putter farther from the body? If you stand farther from the ball, you will putt with more of an inside-out stroke so that you push the ball toward the hole.

If you prefer a more upright lie, you will stand closer to the ball. This position will promote more of a straight back-and-through stroke. You feel the putter staying close to your body, and the stroke is more a direct hit.

How to Choose?

The putter is the one club for which the golfer's strength and ball-striking ability do not count. It is also the club with which a consistent level of performance is hardest to maintain. It is possible for a high handicapper to putt like a professional and vice versa. That would be impossible with the driver or just about any other club in the bag. Rather than your ability, you need to consider your style of putting to select the right club for you.

Hands Behind The Ball

If you have your hands behind the ball, you strike the ball with a low, then up and through motion. You need a putter with a shaft that angles back from the clubhead. Your putter also needs a flat face so that the ball stays on the ground and rolls as you intend it to.

Hands In Line With The Ball

If your hands are set up in line with the putter head, your stroke should be perfectly symmetrical: backswing, slightly up, striking the ball, follow-through, slightly up. The center-shaft blade, which has the clubhead and the shaft in perfect alignment is the club for you. Make sure you also get a little bit of loft because of the slight downward motion of the putter head at impact.

Hands Ahead Of The Ball

If you have your hands ahead of the ball at address or begin your stroke with a slightly forward press, your backswing is higher, you are hitting down on the ball with a lower follow-through. Putters with offset hosels which account for the majority of models available, are designed for you. Because of your downward stroke, you also need more loft so that the ball is not hit into the ground and caused to bounce.

UTILITY CLUBS

The elegant, matched set of clubs with three woods and ten irons has long been the popular choice of golfers, but today more and more of them are customizing their basic set by adding new clubs and replacing old ones until they get the set that best matches their playing abilities and course conditions.

Utility clubs are designed to perform specific tasks and broaden your range of shotmaking. While most utility clubs make a lot of sense, you will have to make a choice by exclusion, or else you may easily end up with 18 or more clubs in your bag.

Three, four or five woods are standard today, you may also want to add a trouble-shooter to hit out of the rough, then your set of irons, not to forget the putter, specialty wedges and maybe a chipper — all that adds up to a lot of weight and probably many more clubs than your bag can hold or the Rules of Golf allow.

I recommend you rather add more woods, and leave your long irons at home, unless you can handle them very well. And, if you want to listen to my advice, consider carrying three wedges in your bag. They are a big bonus for almost any player anywhere.

5-Woods

Probably the most popular utility club in the bag is the 5-wood. Today, most standard sets come with a 5-wood rather than a 4-wood, and rightfully so. I believe that virtually all golfers should carry a 5-wood. It is easy to use and it is versatile, because you can use it on the fairway and in the short rough, and even off the tee on longish par three's.

The 5-wood is designed to hit the ball about as far as a 3-iron. With an angle of about 25° it has more loft than the iron, but its longer shaft allows you to create more clubhead speed resulting in a higher, softer shot compared to the lower, boring flight of the 3-iron with more roll.

A variation of the 5-wood comes with two rails on its sole running from front to back. It first emerged in the mid 1970s when Cobra Golf marketed the Baffler. The rails allowed the club to skid rather than dig into the turf, making it easier to hit out of the rough.

If you belong to the vast majority of golfers who cannot hit their long irons high, then the 5-wood is a necessity. Even Raymond Floyd carried a 5-wood when he won the 1976 U.S. Masters. He used it to hit high, soft approaches to Augusta National's back-nine par five's, shooting a total of 271, 17 under par, and equalling Jack Nicklaus' tournament record.

7-Woods

More recently, clubmakers introduced the 6-wood and the 7-wood. The latter is widely used for trouble-shots out of the rough, where height and distance are important.

Lee Trevino, one of golf's great shotmakers, carries a 7-wood in his bag, because it allows him to hit high, floating shots with his regular swing, which usually generates rather low trajectories.

With the 7-wood, you can let the club do the work. You can make a good, solid contact, and the club will get the ball in the air. Like the 5-wood, the 7-wood also comes in the rail-soled version to help with the shots out of the deeper rough.

1-Irons

Although this long accuracy club is far more common today than it was several years ago because more golfers are able to hit the perimeter-weighted model than the earlier blades, it is a utility club for good amateurs and professionals only.

The very best players use this flat-faced club with only 16° or 17° loft to hit the ball about as far as their 3-wood, but much more accurately, because the shaft of the iron is about three inches shorter than that of the wood. While the 1-iron may be hit from the fairway, it is mainly used as a driving iron on short, tight par four's. Some golfers use it also to keep the ball in play on long par five's.

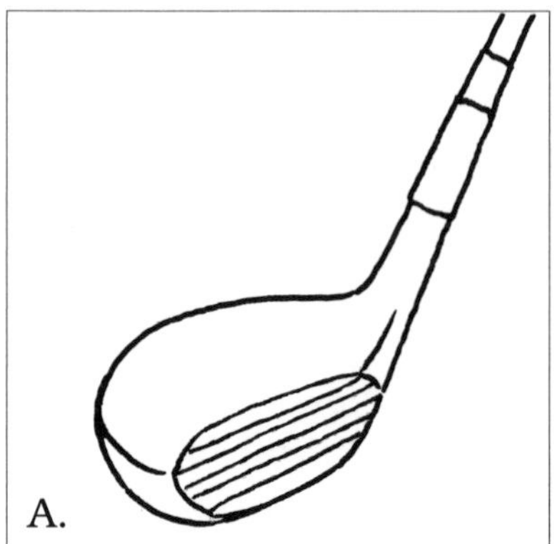

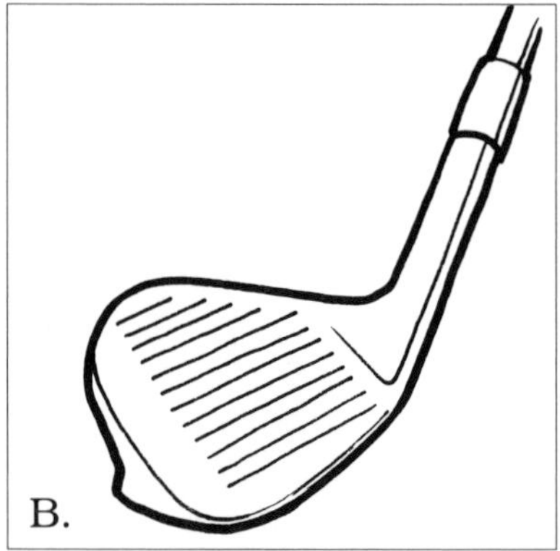

A. The 7-wood has become one of the preferred utility clubs. B. The sand wedge with a short flange can accomplish more than bunker shots. C. The chipper is for players who cannot hit a chip-and-run shot with their mid irons.

Despite the advancement of technology, the 1-iron is still the hardest club in the bag to hit consistently well. Unless you are an excellent ball striker, you are far better off with a full complement of woods.

Pitching Wedges

I have always advocated carrying three wedges on the course: a pitching wedge of about 50° loft, a sand wedge of around 55° loft, and a lob wedge of roughly 60° loft.

The approach shot with a three-quarter or half swing is one of the toughest to judge. Tournament professionals practice approach shots as much as any other to get the feel for the right amount of power they need. The pitching wedge and the new lob wedge are designed for these high, soft shots.

You can make a full swing with them even for the short approach shot, imparting more backspin on the ball, causing it to land more softly on the green and to stay there. As the lob wedge has already more loft than regular wedges, you don't have to open the clubface when you get closer to the hole.

Many tournament professionals now carry lob wedges, and so should you. Although most club players tend to neglect the short approach shot when practising, they encounter it quite often on the course, especially if there are a number of high, small greens on it. As such, the lob wedge is a necessity rather than an option.

Sand Wedges

A good sand wedge must have a lot of bounce, a trailing edge that lies lower than the leading edge, and a rather broad sole allowing you to get the ball out of the sand quickly, without digging in too deeply, and preventing fluffed shots.

Bounce is the main difference between sand wedges and pitching wedges, making the former very difficult to pitch with on firm fairways. It is designed to bounce off these, resulting in a thinned shot.

While most sand wedges come with broad soles, the good golfers prefer rather narrow soles, because these clubs allow more precise and better controlled shots, since you can hit closer to the ball, imparting more backspin.

When choosing a sand wedge you have to keep the conditions on your home course in mind. The softer the sand, the more bounce you need and the broader the sole should be, and vice versa.

As bunker shots usually require finesse, many tour players, including myself, fit flexible shafts to their sand wedges. This way, you can just use your hands and let the club do the work. For the same reason, your wedge shouldn't be too heavy. Watch out, as a lot of them are.

Chippers

Chipping irons come with a shaft that is about as long as that of a putter and the loft of a 5-iron. They are designed for chip-and-run shots from the apron or the vicinity of the green when you have a lot of green to cover.

Chipping irons allow the golfer to play high percentage shots which will get the ball close to the hole in most cases. However, the chipping iron is an extravagance, as you may have to leave another club at home to keep to the allowed maximum. You should be able to produce the same shots with your mid irons.

How to Choose?

To select the utility clubs you need, you must consider your playing abilities as well as the conditions you normally play under. Here are some pointers.

The High Handicapper

You should consider carrying four woods, driver, 3-wood, 5-wood and a 7-wood, 4-iron to pitching wedge, sand wedge and lob wedge. There is a huge variety of clubs on the market and by mixing and matching, you will put together a set of clubs tailored to your skill and style. Get the right combination and you will save a lot of strokes.

The Mid Handicapper

Your needs are driver, 3-wood, 5-wood, 3-iron to pitching wedge, sand wedge and lob wedge.

The Low Handicapper

If you are a very good low marker of handicap four or less you may carry a 1-iron. What you must consider is if you have the ability to hit the 1-iron consistently well and whether the course you play has narrow fairways which call for high-percentage tee shots. If not, carry a driver and 3-wood, 2-iron through to pitching wedge, conventional sand wedge and lob wedge. Add your putter and you have 14 clubs. If you are playing to a high single figure handicap, you should drop your 2-iron and add a 5-wood.

TEST EQUIPMENT

Many club professionals and specialist golf shops now have test equipment available. Try them. Playing with a club is the best way of knowing if you really like it.

Where possible, obtain a full set of clubs to take to the practice range and to play a round. Keep in mind, however, that not even this is foolproof, because test clubs are usually set to standard specifications and a number of these may not suit you. In all likelihood you will need either different lies on your clubs, different shafts, and different grips but the test set is an excellent starting point.

From there the professional can advise you on what specifications you need. Ideally, he should accompany you on the practice range as you try the test clubs. You can then decide what course of action to take:

- If you are a golfer with an ingrained swing fault and you have neither the time nor inclination to change you will want clubs which minimise the effects of that fault.

- If you are a golfer who is willing to work hard to rectify the fault you will want clubs that in the long term will suit your new swing.

Lie Board

An important piece of equipment used by the professional is the lie board, a device that tells you whether your clubs are set with the right lie, the angle at which the shaft enters the clubhead.

For example, at the address position, you may hold your hands quite low and it may seem that your clubs should be set, say 2° flat, but at impact you may be in a more upright position.

The lie board has a section on which you stand while under the clubhead is a sheet of heavy-duty plastic. Tape is placed on the bottom on the clubhead and you hit a ball from the plastic. Use a club with the standard lie. If the tape marks in the middle of the blade, then standard is right for you; towards the heel means you need a flat lie; towards the toe means you need an upright lie.

When you have been fitted with your new clubs, you should go back to the practice range and try the lie board again to double-check if the set up is right or needs fine tuning.

Having the right lie on your club is imperative. If it is too upright, the heel of the club hits the ground first, opens the clubface through impact and increases the chance of pushing or slicing the ball. If the lie is too flat, the toe hits the ground first, pivots around the heel and increases the chance of hitting a pulled or hooked shot.

Look at the Options

When using test sets, don't just think in terms of the generic combinations like three woods, nine or ten irons and putter. Look at the great variety of utility clubs on the market and try out as many as you think necessary.

Above all, be patient. If you have to wait to try out test clubs because someone else is using them, then do so. Give yourself every opportunity to obtain the right clubs and the right combinations.

SECOND-HAND CLUBS

Is second-hand second best? While shiny, new clubs are certainly an attraction, all you really want is equipment that gets the job done on the course. If you are not going to spend a lot of money, beware of cheap new clubs which may be of poor quality or workmanship. But you could buy a set of second-hand clubs that are well made and can be fitted with good shafts and grips for the same price.

Purchasing second-hand equipment should be the choice of the beginner and the junior player, for they will need to update their equipment soon as their play improves. A junior taking up golf at the age of, say ten, may well need to have his or her clubs upgraded every year.

As good persimmon-headed woods are becoming increasingly rare, many players look through the bargain barrels in pro shops and golf stores, for old woods that are in poor condition, but that can easily be fixed. You could also pick up a good utility club, like a sand wedge or putter, simply by having a good look around.

Most golfer buy new clubs when their equipment starts showing signs of wear and tear. Often this is the wrong choice.

If you get the opportunity to attend a pro tournament, go to the practice range and take a peek in some of the players' bags. You'll be amazed at the seemingly poor quality of some of the clubs you see, looking at the clubheads. Old sand wedges and putters and even whole sets of well worn clubs are common.

Professionals select their clubs with lies and lofts to their liking and have top quality shafts and grips fitted to them. And while the overall composition of the club is carefully considered, if you asked any professional what the single most important component of the club is, they would say the shaft.

Amateur golfers on the other hand think of the clubhead as the business end of a golf club, and don't even bother to have new shafts and grips fitted to their clubs regularly. This should be done every three years if you play more than thirty rounds a year. Instead, most players will go out and purchase new gear.

Really, very few clubheads are worn out by that time, and there is a range of services now available to make your old clubs as good as new. A set of stainless steel-headed clubs, which are used by the majority of golfers, will last for years and years. You can easily get your club pro to grind away any nicks and machine-buff the heads.

From there it is simply a matter of having new shafts and grips fitted to your specifications and having the pro check the lies and lofts of each club and adjust them if need be. All of this is not cheap, but it will cost considerably less than purchasing a new set of clubs.

Not all clubheads last indefinitely. Mild steel heads will wear out fairly quickly and while these can be rechromed it may not be enough if the faces are wearing back through play and practice. Soft alloys such as beryllium-copper are also susceptible to rapid wear.

Irons can be regrooved if the faces are worn to a large degree but you must consider the following:

- By this stage your irons are just about at the end of their usefullness, and:

- You must get the regrooving done by an expert who will ensure the grooves adhere to the Rules of Golf.

With woods, it is the same story, although there are more golfers who have their woods renovated because it is a simpler process. Returning a wood to as-new condition is often a matter of sanding back the head, applying some wood stain or paint and dipping it in the right clear varnish. Fit a new shaft and grip and have the binding replaced and your club will look like one from the showroom. As the market continues to be flooded with metal woods, it is worth your while to keep your persimmon.

CLUB MAINTENANCE

Looking after your playing equipment is necessary to extend the life and resale value of your clubs and to improve their playability. The basics to good club maintenance are neither time consuming nor difficult.

Heads

Keeping the grooves on the clubface free of dirt is important. The grooves are designed to grip the ball at impact and therefore impart more backspin. If the grooves are filled with dirt, backspin is reduced.

The other aspects of care depend on the material from which the clubheads are made.

Hard-wearing stainless steel heads require very little maintenance, other than keeping them clean. When the finish becomes dull, you can have them machine buffed to look as new.

Mild steel needs more care because the chromed clubhead is susceptible to rust. As soon as you detect rust spots, you should remove them with steel wool or a fine sand paper or, better still with a cream cleanser used for enamel surfaces in kitchens, and a small scrubbing brush. This will remove the rust with the least amount of abrasion to the clubhead. A coat of iron oil protects the heads temporarily.

You should not leave your golf bag in the trunk of your car longer than necessary. If you have been playing in wet conditions and your equipment is damp, humidity can build up in the trunk of the car and cause the clubheads to develop rust more quickly.

Wet weather also poses a problem for wooden-headed clubs. Make sure you dry them properly before putting the head cover back on. If the inside of the cover becomes damp, it is best to leave it off altogether, otherwise moisture can soak into the clubhead and cause the wood to swell.

If the head covers are off, be careful when taking other clubs out of your bag to avoid bumps in the wood and marks on the head. Wood oil keeps the heads from cracking if the veneer flakes off, but revarnishing them is the better option.

Shafts

The common chromed mild steel shaft will corrode. Any rust should be removed in the same way I recommended for mild steel clubheads.

Moisture can get trapped in steel shafts when you play in wet weather and water settles inside the bottom of your golf bag. The butt end of the grip gets wet and as you turn the club up to take your address position for the shot, small amounts of water can run down through the hole at the top of the grip and into the shaft, starting corrosion inside.

If the hole in the grip hasn't been sealed off with adhesive tape when the grip was fitted you can prevent the steel shafts from rusting inside by putting tees in the tops of all your grips to keep them above any water that may be in your bag. Even if the grips do get wet, no water will run down the shaft.

Corrosion is not a problem with graphite shafts but the coating can wear off where the shaft rubs on your bag. This doesn't affect the performance of the shaft in any way but will reduce the club's resale value. If you carry graphite shafts choose a golf bag with a padding on the rim and dividers to stop the shafts wearing.

Titanium shafts are maintenance-free. They don't rust and don't wear.

Grips

Grips become slippery because of a build up of grit, putting a shiny coating over the rubber, leather or synthetic.

All you need is soapy water and a small scrubbing brush to clean the grips regularly, after every two or three rounds of golf. Removing the dirt will give the grips the tackiness they had when new.

Gadgets

Among the useful gadgets on the market are pitchforks, which are used to repair pitch marks on the green and to clean the grooves of your clubs. A tee will serve both purposes but the bladed edge of this pitch fork is more effective.

One of the best inventions I've seen is a tube filled with water and detergent, which has a small brush attached, and clips onto your bag. You just give the plastic tube a slight squeeze, and you can clean the clubhead or grip, or your shoes for that matter.

They are particularly good if you have cavity-backed irons as the brush will remove any debris from the back of the clubhead. The tubes are inexpensive, durable and very effective.

At the very least you should carry a towel with you when you play golf, keeping one end damp so you can clean your golf balls or clubs along the way.

Golf Bags

You want a bag that will house your clubs safely without having them jammed in. A bag with a club compartment of nine inches in diameter will meet your needs although you can get up to an 11-inch bag. Make sure the bag has strong stitching, good zippers and enough pockets.

You need one large pocket for additional clothing, wet weather gear and towels, a smaller one near the base of the bag for golf balls, another for tees and yet another for wallets, car keys and tubes of sun screen. Near the top should be another small pocket in which you can keep your scorecard and gloves.

The club compartment should be divided into six sections. Some bags have padded dividers running down to the bottom of the bag which is particularly important if you have graphite-shafted clubs, as the coating on the shaft will wear on vinyl dividers, while the ferrules, the caps where the shafts enter the hosel of the club, can be marked over a long period.

Most large bags are made from heavy-duty vinyl which is long wearing, waterproof, and easy to clean. While leather was the preferred choice some years ago, not many bags are made from it these days because of the prohibitive cost and need for regular conditioning of the leather.

With a diameter of six or seven inches, lightweight bags can make a tight squeeze for your clubs and damage the grips. They are also susceptible to being cut and ripped. They are not waterproofed either.

It is a good idea to get a coverall, which protects your bag on trips. These are made from vinyl or canvass. If your budget allows you can purchase a solid plastic carry case. The coveralls increase the life of your bag and reduce the amount of cleaning you need to do.

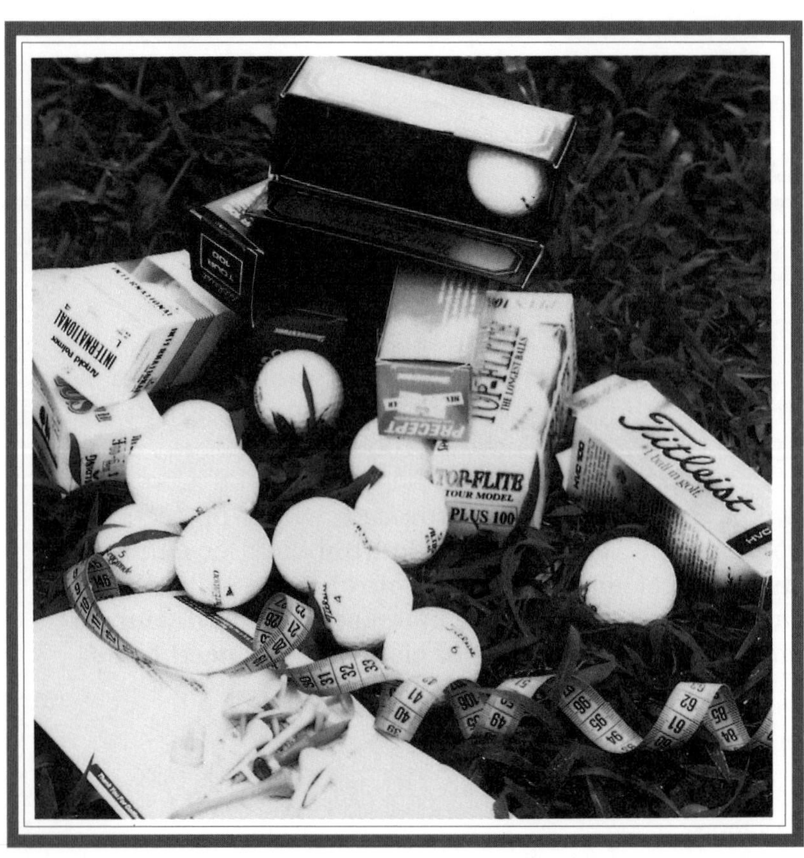
TOP-FLITE
TOUR MODEL
PLUS 100
Titleist

GOLF BALLS

Few golfers are creatures of habit when it comes to selecting the right golf ball. Many will have their preferred choice but if they think a new ball will provide even the smallest advantage, they'll try it.

About one billion golf balls are produced each year in hundreds of different dimple patterns and materials, although the Rules of Golf appear to leave little room for such variety in their strict definition of balls. According to the Royal and Ancient, golf balls must measure at least 1.68 inches in diameter and weigh at least 1.62 ounces. They may not travel faster than 250 feet per second initially and not farther than 280 yards.

Developments

This is a far cry from the production of the original ball, the feathery, stitched leather stuffed with a hat full of wet feathers, which hardened as it dried. Thought to be first made around 1400, the feathery was in use until the gutta-percha, a one-piece ball made from Malaysian tree sap, was developed towards the middle of the 19th century.

The gutta-percha had a smooth surface and it was found that when the ball was cut and nicked it performed better. This led to the development of the hand-hammered gutta which was given a patterned surface and became the forerunner to the modern, dimpled ball.

For more than a half-century, the only type of golf ball available was the three-piece with solid core, rubber windings and balata cover. Basically, it was a ball which suited the best golfers but was used by everyone. Obviously, there was room for improvement and appeal to the mass market. The surlyn-covered ball was introduced and it proved a boon for the club golfer.

It was durable, with its cover virtually cut-proof under normal playing conditions, and because of its hardness, provided lower spin rates, the result of which was a ball that flew farther and deviated less when hooked or sliced.

The hard-covered balls, whether two-piece or three-piece, became the preference of just about every club golfer the world over. That began to change in the early 1980s with the development of long-distance balatas. Titleist's 384 Tour Balata broke new ground.

Dimples

Titleist's success lay not in the cover material but in aerodynamics due to the ball's dimple patterns. The 384 (for the number of dimples), with customized pattern, was achieving about six yards more carry than other balata balls, although tour professionals claimed at the time they were hitting the ball 20 to 30 yards farther. In a twinkling there was a proliferation of extra-dimple golf balls with some having well in excess of 400 dimples. The number, it seemed, was not important as long as it was more than 384. It was a matter of more dimples, more distance.

It is questionable if the proper research was done, if the "more is better" theory worked, if the dimples were the right width, the right depth, the right configuration. But each new ball on the market was proclaimed to travel farther, even if only a few yards, or feet.

Golf balls have just about reached the limit of 250 feet per second initial velocity which is governed by the Rules of Golf. The makers already have the technology to manufacture balls that would have the average golfer hitting drives 300 yards and the touring professional around 400 yards, but sensibly this is illegal as it would make a nonsense of golf courses.

Now, with improvements in distance being measured in such small increments, the interest by manufacturers is in playability.

Backspin

Most people think that only the best golfers can hit the ball with a lot of backspin. But really anyone with sound technique can do it, although some can do it better than others.

In general, low backspin sends the ball on a low trajectory, with a long roll. If you hook or slice, it will

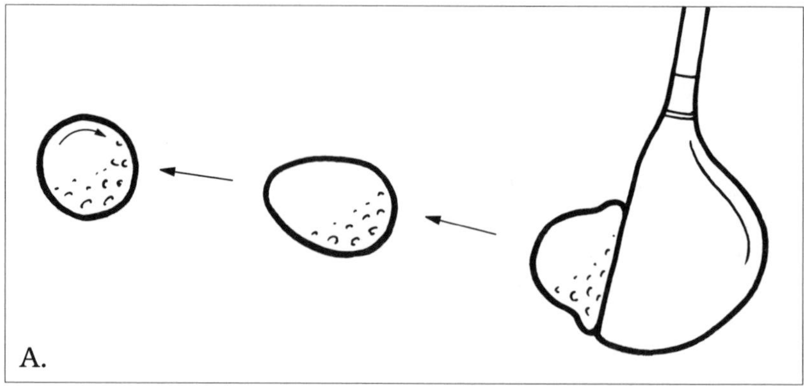

A. This is a grossly exaggerated version of the distortion at impact, but something like this actually happens every time you hit a ball. In reality, the clubface doesn't remain straight either. The energy released at impact turns into a backspin once the ball has regained its shape.

show less with less backspin. High backspin sends the ball on a high trajectory, with less roll. If you mis-hit the ball, the problem will be aggravated.

Greg Norman is an excellent example of a golfer who can impart more backspin than just about anyone because he attacks the ball from such a steep angle on his downswing. Nick Faldo is an example of a golfer with a flatter swing plane and less vigorous release.

Now, having said that, let me add that Faldo certainly has the ability to impart enough backspin. In truth, every shot in golf begins its journey with backspin, even a putt. What produces maximum backspin is the club striking the ball a descending blow and the effect is accentuated by how steep the angle is, the speed of the clubhead and the loft of the club. A wedge imparts more back spin on the ball than any other club. There are other contributing factors:

- If the ball is in the rough and grass gets between the clubhead and ball at impact, this will markedly reduce the ability to impart backspin. This is a major contributing factor.

- Clubhead material, whether mild steel or soft alloy or the harder stainless steel, has an effect. No matter what material the clubhead is made from, the ball stays on the clubhead for an instant at impact. With mild metals it stays there longer and as such more backspin is imparted. Clubhead material, however, is a minor contributing factor.

All the major golf ball manufacturers conduct tests but their findings vary greatly because of the conditions applied.

Here are some samples spin rates in revolutions per minute:

	Three-Piece Balata	Three-Piece Surlyn	Two-Piece Surlyn
Driver	3,500	3,000	2,500
5-Iron	7,000	6,500	5,500
Wedge	9,500	9,000	8,000

While the differences in initial spin rates may seem minor, they have a marked effect on landing. The balata, for instance, will land more softly and will stop more quickly.

Compression

For many years, golf balls of different compressions have been available. Compression is the measure of how much the ball distorts at impact.

When the clubface meets the ball, both ball and clubface are distorted. Since the ball is softer, it is flattened against the clubface. As it recovers its original shape, the energy of the distortion is transformed into speed.

The lower the compression, the softer the ball and the more it distorts. As such a ball with low compression is designed to help the player who cannot generate much clubhead speed. Basically, ladies use an 80 compression ball, the average male golfer 90 compression and the power hitter 100 compression.

The number on the ball that marks the compression is an approximation. A nominal compression, of say 80, refers to a real compression of 80 to 90, while a nominal compression of 100 would lie between 100 and 110. Compression again affects backspin. The difference between the 90 and the 100 compression version of the same ball model can range from 200 to 500 revolutions per minute.

Three-Piece Balata

This ball is the favourite of the professionals, because it comes with a lot of natural backspin. Its solid core wound in rubber was originally covered with a substance between resin and rubber, which was harvested from various trees of the sapodilla family in South America.

Although today, most manufacturers substitute the natural balata with synthetic, the playing performance of the ball remains. The balata will stop faster on the green and has a softer feel when putting. With the long game it can be worked more from left to right or right to left and it reacts better with finesse shots.

The major disadvantages are loss of distance and lack of durability because the cover will be cut and scuffed with thinned shots when the leading edge of the clubhead hits the centre of the ball.

The points you need to consider if you want to use balata are:

CHECKLIST

✔ Do you hit the ball far enough? A balata ball does not go as far as a surlyn ball.

✔ Do you have any trouble controlling the ball? A balata ball, because it achieves more backspin, is harder to control. Any hook or slice is accentuated.

✔ Can you make a balata ball work for you? The balata ball is designed to be finessed, the only advantage being for shots to and around the green. You can make a balata ball stop more quickly but only if you have the ability. It's like owning a pair of spiked running shoes when all you have the ability to do is jog. Your sneakers, obviously, are more practical.

✔ Are you prepared to spend more? Balata balls are priced at the top end of the market, and because they are less durable they have to be replaced more often. Touring professionals, for instance, use balatas and change them about every three holes during tournament play. You may get a full round out of one, but chances are you won't. The hard-covered models may last for two or three rounds.

Leading Brand Golf Balls

	MODEL	CONSTRUCTION	COMPRESSION
HIGH SPIN Low Handicappers	**Bridgestone Rextar Pro**	3-piece-balata,wound liquid centre	90 and 100
	Dunlop Maxfli HT	3-piece-balata,wound liquid centre	90 and 100
	Ram Tour	2-piece, lithium balata cover	90 and 100
	Spalding Tour Edition	2-piece, zinthane cover	90 and 100
	Titleist Tour	3-piece-balata, wound liquid centre	90 and 100
MID SPIN Mid Handicappers	**Dunlop CD**	3-piece, lithium cover, wound rubber centre	90 and 100
	Spalding Top Flite Tour	2-piece, zylin cover	90 and 100
	Titleist DT	3-piece, lithium surlyn cover, wound rubber centre	80, 90 and 100
	Wilson Staff TC	3-piece, surlyn cover,wound rubber centre	90 and 100
LOW SPIN High Handicappers	**Bullet DFS**	2-piece, surlyn cover	95
	Dunlop Maxfli MD	2-piece, surlyn cover	90 and 100
	Spalding Top Flite XL	2-piece, zylin cover	90 and 100
	Titleist MVC	2-piece, lithium surlyn cover	90 and 100
	Pinnacle Gold	2-piece, lithium surlyn cover	90 and 100
	Pinnacle	2-piece, surlyn cover	90 and 100
	Wilson Ultra	2-piece, surlyn cover	90 and 100

If your answer to any of the above is "No", then look for something else.

One ball which has the same performance characteristics as the three-piece balata but is of two-piece construction is Spalding's Tour Edition. It has a solid core and a zinthane cover. Zinthane is an elastic material, softer than surlyn, allowing a high rate of backspin, but it doesn't cut like balata when mis-hit.

Two-Piece with Blended Cover

A new mid-range ball has only just emerged onto the market. It is designed to provide more backspin than the conventional long-distance, surlyn-covered balls but less than balata models. There is little trade-off in distance and some manufacturers claim it is just as long as the hard-covered models.

The development of the ball has been made possible through the application of new cover blends, whether it be a thinner surlyn, one such as lithium-surlyn or a new compound altogether. Spalding, for instance, has a unique material called zylin for its new Top-Flite Tour ball. It is designed to feel softer than surlyn, be more reactive at impact and produce more backspin.

Three-Piece with Surlyn Cover

This was the first attempt by manufacturers to produce a mid-range ball with the wound centre giving the ball a softer feel while the surlyn cover offered durability and maintained a lower spin rate than balata.

Two-Piece with Surlyn Cover

Designed for the majority of golfers, this ball offers two overriding advantages – greater distance and durability. Because it reacts less than any other ball, the two-piece surlyn varies less in flight and travels farther.

What Ball Should You Use?

In comparison to professionals, club golfers, more so mid to high handicappers, are less aware of their requirements and as such are more likely to experiment to the point where this becomes a never-ending process because there are so many new golf balls coming onto the market.

In most cases this has little effect, for if a golfer stays within a certain category, say the two-piece surlyn-covered range, he or she will not notice much difference. However, if you want to switch to a ball with substantially different spin and flight characteristics you have to weigh up the aspects of your own play and your ability on the way to making the right choice. When choosing the golf ball you will play with, you should try to match your ability with the playing characteristics of the ball. The vast majority of golfers should not use the soft cover models because the disadvantages outweigh the advantages.

The High Handicapper

The balata ball is not the ball for you. You need a ball that is easier to keep in play. Because of the lower rates of backspin of surlyn-covered balls their flight is less erratic and longer when played by golfers who exert less control and power over their shotmaking. While there are no strict guidelines, you should use the two-piece surlyn.

The Mid Handicapper

The average player is well advised to use the three-piece surlyn ball. However, this is a very broad classification and the main variable is feel. If you feel comfortable and confident using a certain type of ball, then play with it.

The Low Handicapper

As a good golfer, you should have a look at the new mid-range balls. With a low single-figure handicap a balata ball may tempt you.

Conditions

Another major variable, and one I don't think enough golfers take into consideration, is the conditions you are playing in.

- You are an average golfer and your local course has

hard, fast greens. It may be wise to use a softer ball, say a three-piece surlyn as opposed to the two-piece you are used to playing with. The three-piece has a softer feel, offers more backspin and will stop better on your approach shots. The loss of distance may be worth the extra control you will have around the greens.

- A lot of rain has fallen in your local area and the fairways and greens have become soft. Even if you are a low-handicapper who normally uses a balata ball, it would be wise to play with a hard-cover model. What you need under heavy conditions is distance. If the greens are soft, whether you use balata or surlyn your approach shots will stop. The playability of balata and need for finesse shots are negated.

There is a lot to golf ball selection. By all means experiment but above all there is one question you must ask yourself: "Does the ball I'm using fit the way I play the game?" If it does, it will help your golf.

Dolgellau
Barmouth
The Bar

GOLF SHOES

The right footwear is as important as the clubs you use for if you do not have a good grip on the ground, then neither the right playing equipment nor a good swing can help.

The weight distribution and thus the pressure points on feet and shoes vary from player to player, from professional to high handicapper, and from left hander to right hander. And, of course, they change throughout the different phases of the swing.

The weight should be rather evenly distributed between both feet at address, with just a little more weight on the heels. The right hander then shifts the weight to the inner side in front of the right foot during the backswing while some weight remains in front of the left foot. The weight settles on the outer side in the middle of the left foot at impact, and puts some pressure back at the front right foot during the follow-through. For the left hander, the opposite is true.

It is on these pressure points that you need the most support from your shoes. As the danger of slipping is greatest when the weight pressure is highest, this is also where the spikes or rubber tips should be located on the soles of your golf shoes.

Your golf shoes should be snug without being too tight, the type that gives you plenty of feel, so that you can feel how your weight is distributed when you take your stance. You certainly don't want a shoe which is even a little bit too big, for while it may be comfortable your feet will move around inside the shoe and this affects your balance throughout your swing.

How do you go about selecting the type of shoe you want? The things you must consider are conditions in which you play golf, the look of the shoe, its life expectancy and your budget. While you may not wish to outlay a large sum, the idea is to get value for money.

There are hundreds of designs now available and generally the quality of golf shoes is very good. Wide research and development and the use of new, lightweight materials have revolutionized golf shoe design with the player reaping the benefits. I will outline the types of shoes available and the suitability of each.

All-Leather Classics

These are the most expensive shoes on the market but they come with the manufacturer's guarantee of great comfort, durability and a better look. Most all-leather shoes are made with the upper stitched to the sole, which is still the most reliable way of making shoes. They are made from the best and softest leathers and have a soft calf-leather lining.

Almost all tournament professionals, and a fair portion of the golfing population, wear this type of shoe because they have the stylish appearance of a good street shoe and are available in a wide range of colours and styles.

The all-leather classic will last for years, if you look after them, and be comfortable throughout. While their price is high, these shoes do offer very good value for money. The all-leather classics may last two or three times as long as the cheaper lines.

Any shoe with a leather upper should feel just a little bit tight when new, so you may need to place bandaids on those parts of your foot which blister when wearing new shoes.

If you want a lightweight shoe, look for something else because the all-leather brands are the heaviest on the market.

Mixed Classics

The leather shoes with synthetic sole and lining are very popular because they have the classic look of the all-leather shoes, while offering several advantages over them. These shoes are cheaper, they are lighter and they do better in bad weather. Although a number of brands now actually come with a waterproof guarantee from six months up to two years, obviously this doesn't mean for you to walk through puddles.

The trade-in is durability. These shoes are prone to loose their good looks after a while, because their leather uppers are of a lesser quality. The sole and the

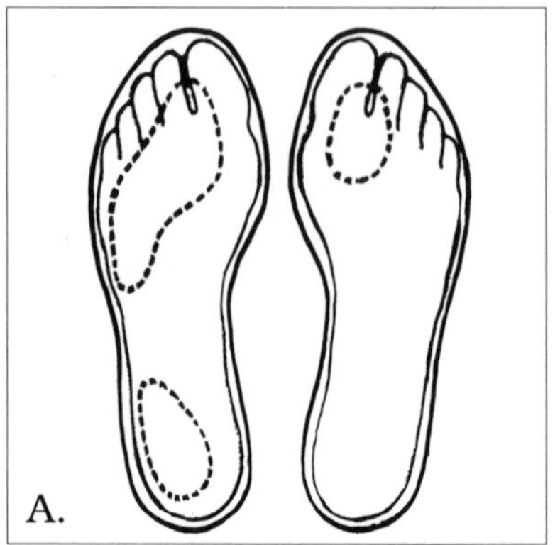

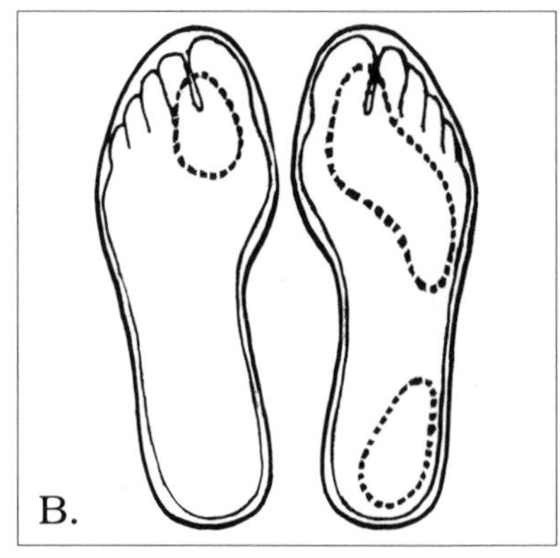

A. This is the weight distribution of a right hander at impact with the weight concentrated on the front left foot, while the right foot shows hardly any pressure.

B. The reverse is true for left handers.

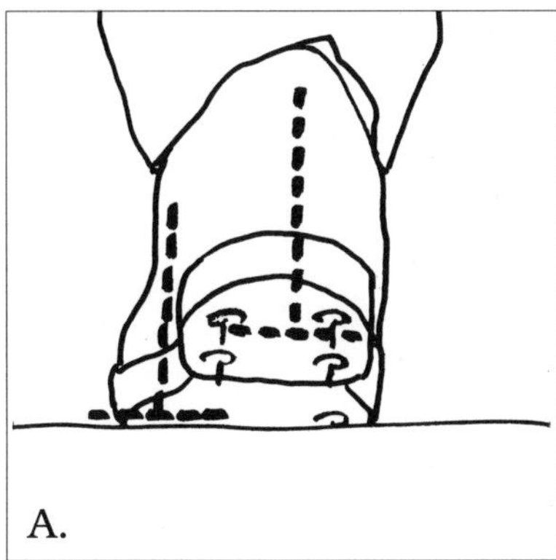

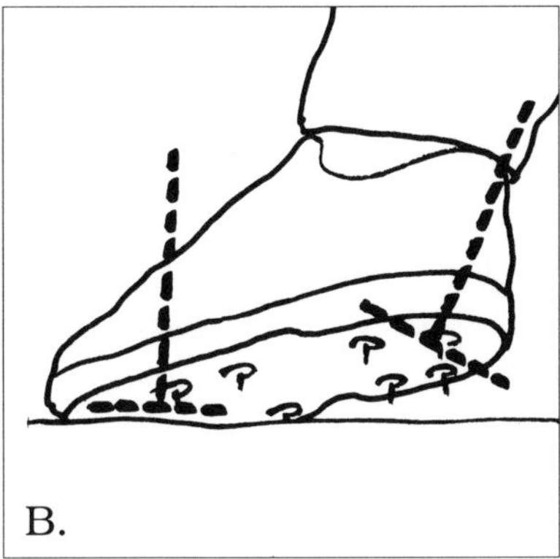

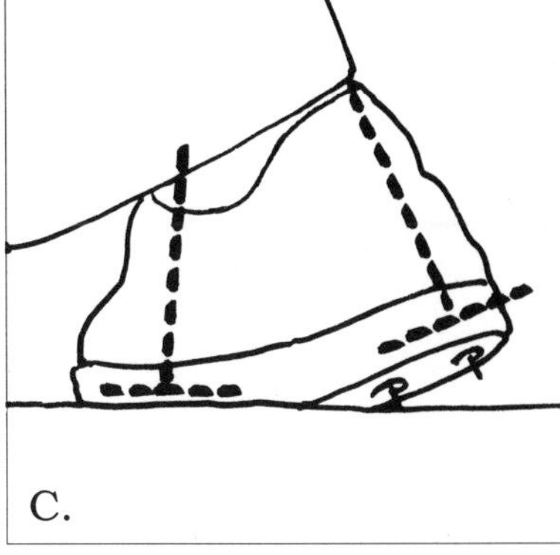

A. The torsion in simple walking is shown here for the right foot. B. This is the torsion of the left foot of a right hander during the backswing. C. The torsion of the right foot at impact.

upper which are glued together rather than stitched may also separate in the long run.

All-Synthetic Classics

New synthetics make these shoes a better proposition today than they were some years ago. The materials used these days won't make your feet sweat as much as they don't seal off the air. The shoes are now quite comfortable, ultra-light, and very good when the fairways are wet. Waterproof guarantees abound.

The synthetics are also easy to clean, requiring nothing more than a wipe over with a damp cloth when you finish your round. They are cheap as well, but they don't last long.

Athletic Shoes

These shoes are in effect tennis shoes with spikes. They are usually light and fitted with a lot of padding, making them the most comfortable shoes in the market. They have synthetic or rubber soles and either synthetic or leather uppers. Again quite a few models carry a waterproof guarantee.

Although inexpensive, some fashion-conscious golfers feel the athletic shoes suit the golf course as much as sneakers the office.

New Designs

With manufacturers from the leisure-shoe industry entering the golf market, comfort has become the biggest selling point for golf shoes. Nike introduced an athletic model featuring an air-pocket inside the sole, while Reebok offers a classic golf shoe with a bladder built into the sole, which can be inflated according to your needs.

Another innovation is the use of graphite and glass fibre inlays in the soles of a number of branded golf shoes. They are designed to flex during your walk, and to resist twisting during your swing. They are also very light.

Spikes

Golf shoes either sport a rippled sole or they have spikes. Rippled soled shoes lead largely a wall-flower existence, probably because quite a number of exclusive golf clubs ban them from their courses alleging that they damage the greens, by tearing the leaves out of the grass. And although more recently it was claimed that they actually do less damage than the spiked shoes, it is the latter that remain the most popular as golfers appear to have become used to them in the past six decades.

More and more golf shoes are now fitted with ceramic-tipped permanent spikes, designed to last as long as the shoe, while making the dirty and cumbersome task of changing spikes obsolete. Ceramic-tipped spikes, which really are metal spikes with a ceramic coating, will in all likelihood also join the long list of materials for replaceable spikes soon, but may turn out to be more expensive than any of those.

The other long-lasting spike material is tungsten, which is also not cheap and has the additional disadvantage of being heavier than steel. Metal-tipped plastic spikes also last quite long, while being substantially lighter than any of the above. However, steel and metal alloys are still the norm for spikes on the market today.

Some shoemakers fit sole ripples in between the patches of spikes to increase grip during the swing.

Whatever your choice of replaceable spikes, you must remove and lubricate the threads before you wear the shoes for the first time. Otherwise you may never be able to change them.

Two or Three Pairs?

There are very good reasons for you to own more than one pair of golf shoes.

- For many golfers, dressing well on the course is very important, because it boosts their confidence. If you are fashion-conscious, you may want shoes of different colours to match your outfits.

- Changing playing conditions may require various types of shoes. You don't want to be wearing your all-leather classics in a downpour. Although the upper may be fairly water-resistant, the soles will soak up the moisture, leading to the eventual deterioration of the stitching, shortening the life of the shoe.

- You want to make sure that you wear white shoes in hot climates, which will keep your feet quite a bit cooler than darker colours.

- You may want to reserve one good pair for tournaments while wearing cheaper or older shoes to the driving range.

- And last but not least, you may want to extend the lifespan of your shoes. If you have just one pair, and play regularly, they will wear out quickly, no matter how good the quality. After wear, a shoe needs one entire day to dry out. If you play golf every day, you have to alternate. You should at least have two pairs of shoes, but I suggest three for the regular player.

Maintenance

Good maintenance of your shoes is very important if you want them to last as long as possible. Different types of shoes require different types of care but all need to be looked after properly.

CARE CHECKLIST

✔ After you have purchased new shoes, **REMOVE THE SPIKES** and **LUBRICATE THE THREADS** before replacing them. This will greatly reduce the chance of the spikes becoming stuck when you need to change them.

✔ After every round, **CLEAN** your shoes properly by wiping them with a damp cloth to remove any dirt and grass clippings. Use a nail brush to remove any impediments from around the lace eyelets and tongue and from between the sole and the upper. Grass in particular will hold moisture.

✔ Use a **SHOE TREE** to keep your shoe in shape, placing it in the shoe immediately after use while the shoe is still slightly damp from perspiration and water. Then it will dry in shape.

✔ If you've played in very wet conditions and the inside of the shoe is saturated, stuff it with **NEWSPAPER** so that it soaks up any excess moisture. This will put the shoe back in shape and avoid the problem of the shoe tree locking in moisture where it is in contact with the inside of the upper.

✔ You must never **DRY** your shoes in front of an open fire or heater. Eventually, this will lead the leather to crack, and if the upper is glued to the sole the parts may unglue in the long run.

✔ Shoes with leather uppers should be **POLISHED** often with a regular polish or an oil-based shoe cream as they help condition the leather. A leather conditioner should be rubbed into the soles and stitching as often as possible. Shoes with synthetic uppers would be cleaned with a light soap.

✔ Make sure your spikes **DO NOT WEAR DOWN**. Those that will wear more quickly are under the ball of your foot and to a lesser degree under the heel. Good spikes will give you a better grip.

GLOVES

Not all golfers wear gloves, but generally the better players do. Fred Couples, the 1992 U.S. Masters Champion is the exception to the rule. But if you have trouble holding the club or feel you are checking it to maintain control, you need a glove.

You will have a better grip of the club when wearing a glove, because it allows you to hold the club with a more relaxed grip, which in turn takes the tension from arms and shoulders and allows you to swing more freely. You also don't have to worry about letting the club slip when your hands perspire.

When purchasing gloves, you will find that the sizes differ greatly from one manufacturer to another even if they bear the same code numbers. Some provide for short, broad hands and fingers, but you must look a long time to find gloves with long, slender fingers.

Don't settle for anything that doesn't fit, and make sure that the fingers in the glove are as long and slender as the fingers on your hand. This is especially true for the thumb and index finger. If your fingers slip around in the glove, you lose your grip, and would be better off to play without a glove.

Leather

Despite its price, the leather glove is by far the most popular, as it provides a softer and more natural feel than the synthetic one. Leather gloves are available in different qualities, and since leather is a natural product, the quality may vary from glove to glove within a particular model.

Leather gloves are fashioned from calf, sheep, goat and even deer hide. While deer skin gloves are the finest and longest lasting, they are scarce and especially expensive. Cabretta, the goat hide, is the second best bet, both in quality and price. Calf hide is not as elastic as cabretta, it has to be cut thicker to withstand the pressure of the club in your hand, and the older the calf, the worse it gets.

The best golf gloves are very soft and thin to give the golfer a better feel. The thicker gloves have a tendency to tear sooner as they are made of a lesser quality leather. They are also more likely to turn hard and brittle from perspiration and rain.

Leather gloves suffer in bad weather. Today, however, many manufacturers treat the leather to repell moisture, increasing the glove's life span and playability. The better gloves now also come with elastic gussets on the back to ensure that they remain in place during play.

If you often play in a warm climate, you may want to look out for gloves with perforated fingers. The resulting air flow will keep your hands cooler and drier, and in turn lengthen the durability of your glove.

Another variety of leather glove shows an imprinted pattern on the palm to give a better grip. These may be worth a try. Some glovemakers even produce gloves with cut-off fingers presumably to allow for a better feel in the fingertips, but I could never figure out why some leather here and no leather there should improve something as subtle as feel.

When you purchase a leather glove, it should feel snug, even a little tight, when you first put it on. The leather will stretch to fit comfortably in good time.

To turn your leather glove into a good proposition in terms of value for money, you will have to take good care of it.

CARE CHECKLIST

✔ Remove your glove between shots so that it doesn't absorb more sweat than necessary and gets a chance to dry.

✔ After golf, store the glove so that it dries slowly away from sunlight and the radiator. If you want to keep it in your bag, make sure the pocket is zipped up and the glove not folded.

✔ In wet conditions, keep two or three gloves in your bag and change them regularly to prevent them from getting soaked.

✔ If a glove is through and through wet, stuff it with paper which will absorb most of the moisture. After that, let it dry slowly. While leather gloves of lesser quality will become useless after such an ordeal, the better cabretta will keep its shape and only needs a thorough rubbing and some leather moisturizer to return to its former suppleness.

Synthetic

Synthetic gloves are designed for golf in bad weather and budget-conscious golfers. The synthetic material is long lasting and washable, doesn't absorb moisture and allows you to maintain a reasonable hold on the club in any condition.

However, there are problems with synthetic gloves. In damp conditions they become uncomfortable, they do not stretch to fit exactly like a leather glove, and because of the harsher fabric they don't offer as soft a feel as a leather glove.

Some manufacturers produce synthetic gloves with leather patches above the thumb pad to give a leather-like feel. But to me this seems to be a gimmick.

SWING TRAINERS

For any golfer the hardest problem to overcome is an ingrained swing fault, one that he or she makes involuntarily because it is committed to what coaches call "muscle memory". Whether you are aware of the problem or not it can be very difficult to rectify because it has become ingrained through repetition and the only way to fix the fault is by repeating the correct technique.

Professional coaches will identify the problem and show you the correct technique but that is only the first step on what can be a long road to fixing your swing.

The golfer must be prepared to heed the professional's advice and practise hard. But when away from the coach's trained eye, you may fall back into the same bad habits or over-compensate. This is where training aids can provide invaluable benefits.

These come in many shapes and sizes, from simple items to elaborate designs but the principle behind them all is the same – to lock you into the correct technique through repetition. You then have the correct "muscle memory", and can rely on your ability on the course.

The type of fault you have governs what type of training aid you require. Don't think you need some wonderful apparatus to fix your problem. You may make do with something as simple as a tee.

Home-Made Trainers

For instance, if you take the club away from the ball wrongly, you can simply put a tee in the ground about two feet behind the ball on the correct line. Swing back towards the tee, and you are using a very effective training aid.

Your feet are wrongly aligned? You need only to place a club on the ground pointing in the right direction. Place your toes just behind the shaft and again you have an ideal guide to the correct alignment.

Let's say your problem is hitting from the top, an action in which you tend to cast your hands away from your body at the start of your downswing, making you chop down on the ball or hit from the outside and across it. Practise by swinging a straw broom to give you the feeling that the club head is lagging behind your hands on the downswing. The wind resistance to the head of the broom will create that feeling which you will then be familiar with when swinging a golf club.

A similar problem with a different remedy. You are hitting from outside to in or from too much on the inside of the target line before impact and outside the line after impact.

A popular training aid is a simple piece of timber, usually 4 x 2 inches thick and about three feet long which is placed just outside the ball, pointing along the target line.

If you hit from the top and the clubhead approaches the ball from the outside, you will hit the timber on the way down. Too much from the inside and you hit the timber after impact. Simple, but brillantly effective. You soon forget about the ball and concentrate on swinging the club properly so that you don't hit the wood.

You may, however, need to use one of the elaborate inventions on the market, and there are a number of very good ones about.

Moulded Grip

As the name suggests, it is a grip which is shaped to make you place your hands in the right position when gripping the club. A number of professionals have these but the problem is catering for golfers with different-sized hands.

It is also unlikely that the club to which this grip is fitted will have the right shaft, lie, weight and loft for you, and so any shots you hit could give you a false impression.

It is better that you know the correct grip position and make sure you stick with the change. Accept the fact that changing your grip is one of the hardest things to do and be prepared to hit a lot of practice balls until you are comfortable.

Full-Swing Trainer

This is an impressive but quite simple device which has a large, circular moulding fitted to an adjustable frame. The golfer stands inside the circle which is angled so that the top of the circle is above and behind your shoulders and the bottom below and in front of your knees.

The circular frame is usually made from a heavy-duty, smooth plastic which allows you to make a normal swing, all the time concentrating on keeping the shaft of your club in contact with the frame. It trains you to swing the club in the right plane and arrive at the ideal position at the top of your swing whereby the clubhead is pointing down the target line.

If the club is coming away from the frame then you are throwing it across the target line. If you feel you are putting too much pressure against the frame then you are letting the club fall away from the target line.

Because the supporting frame is adjustable, the trainer will accommodate golfers of all dimensions.

Harness

Many coaches these days subscribe to the swing principle of keeping your arms close to your body throughout your swing which is the method Nick Faldo uses, hence its popularity.

For those who want to swing this way, a common drill is to place a towel across your chest and hold it in

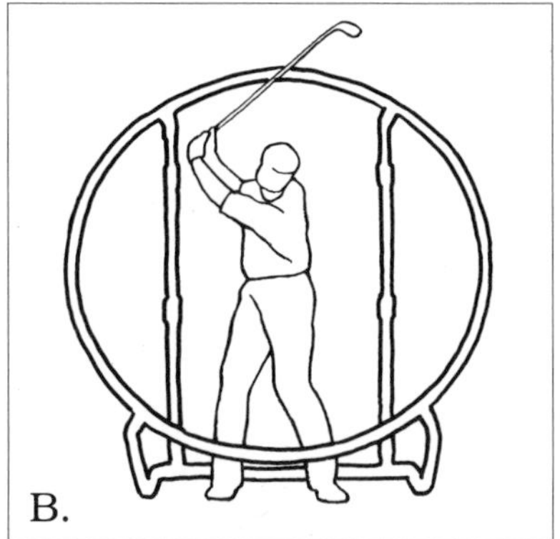

A. The swing trainer may help you to regain what you have lost by guiding you gently towards a better swing. B. The same device is available in a variety of shapes and sizes.

place with your arms throughout the swing.

Taking this a step further is a customized, adjustable belt which is tightened around each arm and across your chest so that no matter how much you try to hit with your arms away from your body, you can't.

Putting Trainers

They have been marketed in recent years to help you develop a sound, repetitive stroke. One popular drill which has been practised by golfers for many years is placing two rows of tees in the ground, leaving you just enough room to swing in between.

What we now see are trainers designed to do the same thing. One developed in Australia, The Puttmaster, has a slightly curved rail near ground level onto which the shaft of your putter is clamped, and you swing along the rail on the correct path.

It can be adjusted to accommodate more than a dozen strokes: inside to out, straight back and straight through, inside to inside and more. You choose the stroke you think is right for you and practise it on the trainer, gradually becoming comfortable with that action.

Another device is a T-shaped frame with a curved cross-bar bending around your chest and held in position under your armpits. You attach the down-bar to your putter shaft beneath your hands. The frame is made of light material and doesn't feel awkward when you stroke your practice putts. The aim is to take any wrist movement out of your putting stroke, making your hands, arms and shoulders work as one unit, which is widely regarded as the most reliable way to putt.

There are many training aids on the market. Those I have mentioned should give you an idea as to what can be used to help your game. Have a look around but make sure you have a good understanding of what the trainer you choose is designed to do. If not, seek the advice of a qualified professional.

QUICK REFERENCE